I0031263

Conversations in Cyberspace

Conversations in Cyberspace

Giulio D'Agostino

BEP BUSINESS EXPERT PRESS

Conversations in Cyberspace

Copyright © Business Expert Press, LLC, 2019.

All rights reserved. No part of this publication may be reproduced, stored in a retrieval system, or transmitted in any form or by any means—electronic, mechanical, photocopy, recording, or any other except for brief quotations, not to exceed 400 words, without the prior permission of the publisher.

As part of the Business Law Collection, this book discusses general principles of law for the benefit of the public through education only. This book does not undertake to give individual legal advice. Nothing in this book should be interpreted as creating an attorney-client relationship with the author(s). The discussions of legal frameworks and legal issues is not intended to persuade readers to adopt general solutions to general problems, but rather simply to inform readers about the issues. Readers should not rely on the contents herein as a substitute for legal counsel. For specific advice about legal issues facing you, consult with a licensed attorney.

First published in 2019 by
Business Expert Press, LLC
222 East 46th Street, New York, NY 10017
www.businessexpertpress.com

ISBN-13: 978-1-94897-670-1 (paperback)
ISBN-13: 978-1-94897-671-8 (e-book)

Business Expert Press Business Law and Corporate Risk Management Collection

Collection ISSN: 2333-6722 (print)
Collection ISSN: 2333-6730 (electronic)

Cover and interior design by Exeter Premedia Services Private Ltd., Chennai, India

First edition: 2019

10 9 8 7 6 5 4 3 2 1

Printed in the United States of America.

Abstract

Conversations in Cyberspace is a collection of insights on the current state of security and privacy in the Internet world, a brief introduction to some of the most used OSINT (open-source intelligence) tools and a selection of interviews with some of the key figures in ICS (industrial control systems), APT (advanced persistent threat) and online/deep web members organizations. This book aims to be an introduction to the relationships between security, OSINT and the vast and complex world hiding in the deep web for both the security professional and the system administrator interested in exploring the today's concerns in database design, privacy and security-by-design, and deep web members organizations including Cicada 3301, the Unknowns, Anonymous, and more.

Keywords

Deepweb; Dark Web; Hacker; Hacktivist; Cybersecurity; Cicada 3301; The Unknowns; Anonymous; Atlayo; Grams; Torch; Hidden Wiki; Tor; Podesta emails; Greg Walton; Cyberspace; Security; Privacy; Cryptography; GCHQ; GDPR; Debian; Linux; Maltego; AI

Contents

Chapter 1   Introduction 1

Chapter 2   Conversations in Cyberspace 19

About the Author 157

Index 159

CHAPTER 1

Introduction

Conversations in Cyberspace is a collection of insights and online conversations (both on IRC chats and encrypted e-mails) on the current state of security and privacy in the online world with a focus on the Deep Web. I have also included a brief introduction to some of the most used open-source intelligence (OSINT) tools and a selection of interviews with some of the key figures in industrial control systems (ICS), advanced persistent threat (APT) and hackers/hacktivists groups.

During the making of this short book, I have quickly realized I had to include interviews and insights from both people involved in the defense side of security and hackers/"crackers" who enjoy the intellectual challenge of creatively overcoming limitations and restrictions of software systems to achieve novel and unexpected outcomes.

The picture that comes out is a fascinating scenario where the cyberspace is becoming remarkably similar to the "physical space"; an increasing amount of people, groups and organizations are getting concerned about privacy, trust and information shared and promote both in the "clearnet" and the so-called "deep web."

This book aims to be an introduction to the relationships between security, open source intelligence and the vast and complex world hiding in the deep web for both the security professional and the system administrator interested in exploring the today's concerns in database design, privacy and security-by-design.

Offensive security, the team that developed the Kali Linux OPS, one of the most popular pen testing operation systems, cleverly summarizes the hacking spirit with the quote "the quieter you become, the more you can hear" borrowed from the 13th-century Persian poet, Jalāl ad-Dīn Muhammad Rumi.

October 31, 2018, Europe

Search Engines

Finding information on the Dark Web is not difficult. There are lists of Dark Web sites, and you will find Dark Internet search engines. The Onion sites provided in search results present challenges not found in a Bing or Google search results list.

The websites may be temporarily offline, a frequent problem with Dark Web Onion websites. Latency can make entering a query, obtaining results, and visiting the site in a results list time-consuming. Google-like response time is the exception.

The rule is to allocate sufficient time for Tor sluggishness. Additionally, the sites in the results list may be operated by law enforcement or an intelligence entity.

If a Dark Website looks too good to be true, approach with caution, registering or downloading content can allow malware in your computer.

We reiterate these warnings because most Bing and Google users are conditioned to enter a question, scan results list, and see websites confident that problematic destinations are filtered out.

Searching the Dark Web requires a more careful mindset. Keep in mind that you can use your sandboxed computing device to access Surface Web and Dark Internet websites.

Hidden Wiki

Among those easy-to-find "navigator" services for the Dark Web is the Hidden Wiki. With Tor up and running, enter the URL http://thehiddenwiki.org/ and click on a link. The selected Dark Web site will appear in the Tor browser.

If you are using the Tor software package, you can click on a link.

The site will display if it is online. Delays for a few Tor functions maybe 50 seconds or more.

The Hidden Wiki provides Onion links to chosen Dark Web sites in various categories.

The Hidden Wiki is another starting point for Dark Internet surfing. If a website does not resolve, you will have to try again later. You may also use the Paste-bin lookup methods described in the previous chapter to find out if a new Onion speech was posted. If the Hidden Wiki does not respond, an alternate supply of directory list is TorLinks in https://torlinkbgs6aabns.onion.

This website features similar categories and a similar number of listings. If your curiosity is participating in Dark Web forums, you may use the list of discussion groups to learn more about the conventions of Dark Internet services. The study team discovered that one has to build a relationship with the community of every forum. Some forums have a crowd-sourced score, like the consumer ratings on eBay or Amazon. The methods vary by Dark Web forum.

Ahmia

The Ahmia search system can be queried without the Tor software installed; however, to access a site, you will need to use your Tor-equipped computing device. The Surface Web URL is https://ahmia.fi; the Onion speech was http://msydqstlz2kzerdg.onion. The Ahmia code is an open source project with a repository on GitHub.

Ahmia, operated from Finland, bills itself as a "search engine for solutions resident on the Tor anonymity network."

The system does not maintain Internet Protocol filters and logs results to knock out child abuse hyperlinks.

The system is integrated with GlobalLeaks and Tor2Web.

The system was created by JuhaNurmi, who is the chief executive of the Finnish company Dignify Ltd. (https://dignify.fi). Dignify offers data mining and cyber security research providing information about drug markets and other law enforcement issues.

At the top of the splash screen is a link to "Statistics." The information, when it is available, is helpful. The index contains links to about 5,000 DarkWeb sites. hmia was a 2014 Google Summer of Code project. The goal was to improve the Ahmia system.

In July 2015, Ahmia published a list of Websites which were made to collect traffic from "real" Dark Web sites. In the summer of 2016, Ahmia has been offline more than it has been online.

Grams

Grams is situated at http://grams7enufi7jmdl.onion. One enthusiast clarified Grams as "the Google of the Dark Web." In a 2014 interview, a Grams' system administrator said Grams utilizes a proprietary search technology which displays results from e-commerce websites as well as other kinds of Dark Websites.

Users can add websites to the Grams system for indexing and inclusion in the system.

Grams does not support index child pornography. The process is operated by what appears to be an Eastern European digital money service. Grams offers unique attributes; for instance, a vendor and product search, and the user-friendly Flow, which enables the use of plain English to locate a specific Dark Web site. In 2015, the study team used Grams to find Pappy Van Winkle whiskey after a major shipment was stolen.

The lack of relevance underscored the issues Grams poses to an investigator.

Grams does a fantastic job of pointing a researcher to complete, free books available on Dark Web websites.

The service does an excellent job of indexing medication-related sites. With the inclusion of the Flow service, it is easy to locate specific Dark Web sites provided that the investigator knows the title of the site.

I have found that Grams was able to yield useful results, but its inclusion of irrelevant, off-topic results generated manual inspection of the result pages necessary. Used in concert with other Dark Internet search systems, Grams is acceptable.

Not Evil

Not Evil, located at https://hss3uro2hsxfogfq.onion, is a re-branding of TorSearch and Evil Wiki. The links are filtered. The relevance algorithm takes into consideration what users click on. Not Evil's operator keeps a low profile. The service does not accept DarkWeb advertising. The system allows a user to start a secure conversation with another not Evil user with a chatbot identified as "Ned," an acronym for not Evil Drone. The not Evil system includes a "chat" function from inside Tor. One can begin a conversation about a query using a chatbot or an anonymous user. Also, not Evil displays the number of items in the index which match the query. Along with the search, the system provides the number of links the not Evil system has indexed. Finally, not Evil provides an application programming interface so that not Evil's performance can be integrated into other applications.

Onion Link

Onion Link can be found at http://onion.city Why is this Dark Web search system interesting is that it appears to use the Google custom search function as well as the Ahmia index to create results? The index comprises links to approximately 20,000 Dark Web sites, depending on the study analysis of Onion Link search results. About six years back, Google operated a Dark Web site, then that website was taken offline. Since that time, Google has not revealed information about its Dark Internet activities. Google did invest in Recorded Future, a company which indexes Dark Internet content. One hypothesis the study team devised was that Google might index some Dark Web content for its research and to support the work of their Google-backed Recorded Future. In late 2016, Google's indexing of glue websites decreased based on our evaluation queries.

Torch

The Torch search system presents a search box, Dark Web advertising, and a link for people wanting to advertise on the Torch system. Notice that when this screenshot was taken, Torch reports that its index contains about 500,000 Dark Web pages, which is about one-third fewer than in other Dark engines. Torch is one of the lower profile Dark Web search programs. One useful feature of the system is term highlighting. The relevancy score produced by the search system makes it easy to spot the frequency of the terms in the indexed site. Results list entries reveal a date where the Torch indexing subsystem visited a site. Torch Dark Web search can be useful. We recommend using it from inside a sandbox.

Free Search Methods

Free Dark Internet search methods provide convenient, easy access to many Dark Web sites. However, none of the systems is without serious shortcomings. The approach I have developed involved crafting a query and then running that query on the five search systems discussed in this chapter. I then downloaded the first five sets of results and merged them. I then visited the Dark Websites which seemed to be most relevant to the specific issue we were investigating. What is obvious is that the time and effort needed to carry out manual queries and results analysis was a burden. There are commercial Dark Internet search systems available to law enforcement, security, and intelligence professionals. Commercial Dark Web search services from Digital Shadows, Recorded Future, and other businesses provide more useful, timely, and accurate DarkWeb search results.

Deep Web Tools

Software like operating systems and popular applications like Web browsers have defects. Programmers can use these issues to put software on a computing device.

The software can arrive via a downloadable file like an image or a document.

Other malware—the typical term for malicious software—offers to install a program, a file, or an image that carries a payload; that is, malware that the unsuspecting user knows nothing about. The malware compromises the user's computing device or a server. The capabilities of exploits and malware are becoming broader and evolving quickly.

One reason is that compromising a user's computer before the data are encrypted sidesteps the barrier of data which must be decrypted. Additionally, software on a user's computer or a Dark Web site's server eases intercepting traffic and eliminates the need for physical access to a user's device.

Terminology can be confusing. Hacking tools are called security suites, penetration testing (pentest) software, or malware.

No matter their labeling, many of these hacking tools in the hands of a programmer can shine a bright light on Dark Web activities.

The software can be utilized in many ways. The study team has identified three widely-used approaches to the use of hacking tools.

Depending on the resources available to an investigative team, the specific solution implemented can include software created by a team member or the department. In several associations, exploit tools are licensed from sellers.

The researchers can deploy the software, often working with the vendor's engineering team. For some instances, a department or investigative team may contract with a third-party firm such as Northrop Grumman or BAE Systems to deal with the work. Malware takes many forms.

Many Deep Web/Dark Web passive collections methods and tools are available. These range from placing the needed code within a computer's operating system or applications to putting malware into the firmware of the computing device. Even though the latter is a more laborious method, some malware cannot be removed or disabled even if the device's memory is erased and a new copy of the operating system installed.

A covert surveillance technique is to set up the malware via a Dark Web session. Many Dark Web users assume their Tor or I2P Dark Internet surfing can't be compromised. That's incorrect. Once the malware is put on the user's computer, the software can intercept and transmit the Dark Web user's information. The Dark Web user's information is transmitted via the Surface Web to avoid the requirement to have special software running on the Dark Internet user computing device. Once installed, the malware conducts its activities invisibly and without changing the lousy actor's computer in a readily visible way. The advantage of this approach to surveillance is that encryption doesn't pose a problem to the investigator. The user's keystrokes are recorded. The data aren't encrypted because the malware captures the Dark Internet user's keystrokes and saves this unencrypted data. An investigator can recreate or "watch" a Dark Web user session. Some malware allows the investigator to start an e-mail, send messages, and initiate transactions without the Dark Web user's knowledge.

The "spoofing" technique utilizes a collection method based on an investigator operating a Dark Internet or Surface Web website. We use the term "spoofing" to refer to an exploit or a set of exploits designed to trick a Dark Web user into visiting a Dark Web site operated by researchers or to supply data to an application or form created by law enforcement to capture personal details. Many variations are available, and new ones are usually introduced. The data input to the spoofed or captured Web site is accessible to the investigator in real time and an unencrypted form. Which Dark Websites are operated by law enforcement? Which are run by bad actors? The research team got a list of about 150 Dark sites which exist in more than one form. A captured Web site could exist online using a distinct Dark Web Onion address. One strategy is to request a secondary and primary e-mail address, a phone number, or a primary and alternate shipping address for orders placed via the site run by law enforcement. More sophisticated methods involve creating mobile applications which appear to be Dark Web applications.

The "multiple exploits method" makes use of a Dark Web site under the control of the investigative team, different infection vectors (forms, applications, E-mail, and so on), and viruses that may migrate from a lousy actor's computer to that of another person known to the bad actor.

Hybrid methods can use applications which spreads through networks. This approach may combine remote-access management of the bad actor's computing device with software designed to perform specific actions when the user of the compromised device is using Signal, an encrypted messaging program, or producing videos for distribution and sale.

If the compromised computer is utilized to keep a Dark Website, the malware can insert itself into the host server and perform specific actions on that remote server. Combined methods make it possible for an investigator to gain access to one or more servers on a network and obtain information germane to a violation of the law across two or more computing devices and their networks.

Citadel

Citadel is an example of a software bundle which includes many features to compromise the Dark Internet user's computer. In 2012, based on SecuLert.com, Citadel's developers offered a variant of this Zeus Trojan as a software-as-a-Service. Citadel is essential since it is an example of an exploit which works from the cloud. The change to cloud-based tools affords many benefits. These include rapid scaling when an exploit succeeds in using digital currencies to help obfuscate the consumer of the exploit. Citadel also contains a social network component.

The consumers of Citadel can contribute new code modules, submit bug reports, and discuss technical issues with other Citadel users. For law enforcement and intelligence specialists to take advantage of Citadel, technical expertise and experience with the software are crucial. Citadel offers different encryption choices.

The software requires a specific botnet key to download malware updates and configuration files, in the hope to not be discovered by trackers. Citadel blocks the choice to download anti-virus and anti-malware tools.

ElcomSoft

Established in 1990, ElcomSoft Co. Ltd is a privately owned company headquartered in Moscow, Russia. Since 1997, ElcomSoft has been actively developing solutions for digital forensics and IT security businesses.

Today, the company maintains a wide range of cellular and computer forensic tools, corporate security, and IT audit products. ElcomSoft products are used by several Fortune 500 corporations, multiple branches of militaries all over the world, police departments, governments, and significant accounting businesses. A complete suite of ElcomSoft password recovery tools enables corporate and government customers to unprotect disks and systems and decrypt files and documents protected with widely used software. ElcomSoft's password recovery applications are fast, but speed depends upon the computer itself and other factors.

The password recovery software makes it easier to access password-protected files in Microsoft Office, Adobe PDF, Zip, and RAR formats. Like most high-end video processing and gaming applications, ElcomSoft uses the video card graphics processing unit to rate some calculations. With the computational load shared between the CPU and the GPU, the time required to recover a password for a protected file is reduced. In addition to the password recovery tool, ElcomSoft offers a Forensic Disk Decryptor, which offers investigators a fast, easy way to access encrypted data stored in crypto containers created by BitLocker, PGP, and TrueCrypt (now discontinued). ElcomSoft can decrypt the entire content of an encrypted volume by mounting the volume as a drive letter in unlocked, unencrypted mode.

EnCase

EnCase has developed among the go-to forensic solutions for a seized device or computer. The program makes it possible for investigators to acquire data and create reports from a wide assortment of devices. Forensic includes a search function to make it easy to ascertain whether particular information is on a device. Forensic can gather information from a range of sources; for example, Webmail, chat sessions, backup files, encrypted files, and smartphones and tablets.

A programmer can use a the Forensic scripting language, EnScript, to automate processes. Search, and investigation or other labor-intensive tasks can be customized using EnScript, which is similar to Java or C++. Forensic generates US court-accepted file formats to validate the integrity of the evidence collected. The system supports most basic file and operating systems. Forensic integrates with optional modules for processing virtual file systems and performing decryption tasks.

Kali Linux

Kali includes over 300 pre-installed tools. Combined with Metasploit, discussed in the following, an investigator with appropriate computer skills can compromise Dark Web users and then make additional inroads into a suspect computer, storage, or mobile device.

Applications acceptable for law enforcement and intelligence work include SQL injection, and denial of service attacks, among others.

SQL injection is a sort of web application security vulnerability in which an attacker can submit a database SQL command that is implemented by a Web application, exposing the back-end database. Kali allows manual methods when access to a user's computer or a server is possible. Kali allows the attack to be mounted using SQLMap, another open source tool. SQLMap simplifies the process of detecting and exploiting SQL injection flaws and carrying over database servers.

Data retrieval from the database and access to the underlying file system is supported. Kali may also be used for blind SQL injection. In this approach, one decides whether a Dark Web site is vulnerable to SQL injection. If it is, a programmer can probe the website to find a database's tables, columns, and records. Once the probe returns a positive result, the programmer can write scripts that iterate through possibilities. Code samples are provided to assist the programmer in using Kali as a stage for blind SQL injection for a single Web site or a group of Web sites of interest to the investigator.

Maltego

Analyzing relationships and displaying the mallows a bird's-eye view of individuals, companies, events, and other entities. The essential notion is that visualization of relationships allows the investigator or analyst to look at information and its interconnections. Instead of pouring through a table of numbers, the Maltego user can spot potentially significant items in chunks of information; for example, linking a telephone number with an e-mail address. Maltego is free for individual users, and the commercial permit fees are a fraction of those for systems available from BAE, IBM, and other firms. You might have seen high-impact visualizations such as this sentiment analysis Twitter messages.

Maltego processes text to recognize and indicator entities such as a domain name, an individual, a company, a phone number, or an e-mail address. The Maltego System uses "transforms" (statistical procedures which relate entities of one type to another type). The outputs provide an intuitive, speedy method to locate specific information, see necessary connections and research individuals who access the Dark Web. The system can generate from content the personal e-mail addresses of people working at a particular government agency.

Metasploit

Metasploit is a collection of hacking software which was initially an open source hacking tool built on the Metasploit Framework.

The hacking tool contains hundreds of modules (software programs). Remote exploits allow the Metasploit programmer to develop applications which can exploit vulnerabilities in browsers, operating systems, and third-party applications like Adobe Flash. The FBI developed its Torpedo applications with Metasploit. The approach utilized by the FBI appears to have exploited Adobe's Flash software. The FBI created a direct connection over the Web; that is, outside of Tor. This link became a pathway for the FBI to collect information about a user.

Nmap

Nmap, or Network Mapper, is a free and open source (license) utility for network discovery and security auditing. Some technical specialists find it useful for tasks such as network inventory, handling service update schedules, and monitoring host or service uptime.

Nmap runs on Linux, Windows, and Mac OS X. It ranks among the top 10 programs on Fresh-meat. Net repository, which contains more than 30,000 programs. The primary goals of this Nmap Project are to help make the Internet a bit more secure and to supply administrators/auditors/hackers with an advanced tool for exploring their networks. Because the complete source code is available, developers can modify Nmap to perform more specialized functions. Nmap processes raw IP packets to determine what hosts are available on the network, what services those hosts are offering, what operating systems (and OS versions) are running, what types of packet filters/firewalls are in use, and dozens of other features.

Nmap involves a command-line Nmap interface in addition to a graphical user interface and results in a viewer (Zenmap), a flexible data transfer, redirection, and debugging tool (Ncat), a utility for comparing scan results (Ndiff), and a packet generation and response analysis tool (Nping).

Nmap is flexible: It supports dozens of innovative techniques for mapping out networks full of IP filters, firewalls, routers, and other obstacles. This includes many port scanning mechanisms (both TCP and UDP), operating system detection, version detection, ping sweeps, and much more. Nmap has been used to scan large networks spanning hundreds of thousands of machines. Nmap is one of the more thoroughly documented forensics tools.

A guide, tutorials and white papers can be found, as well as a developer mailing list (nmap-dev) and a channel on Freenode an EFNet in #nmap.

Open source software is free and supported by a community of users and developers. There's some Dark Web-related applications on GitHub and SourceForge, and you will find freelance programming solutions which make programmers with hacking experience available for hire. A helpful list of Dark Web-centric software was compiled for public access by the Defense.

DARPA

Advanced Research Projects Agency (Darpa) in http://open-catalog. darpa.mil/MEMEX.html. The software was created by researchers, universities, individuals, and commercial organizations. The software wasn't designed to be downloaded and used as a program for an Android or iPhone device. In most cases, the user was assumed to be a programmer.

The program or its constituent elements are no longer publicly available for download via the DarpaMemex directory page. If you find one of the Memex apps, you have the task of assembling the code into operational programs or weaving a module to another piece of software. In Annex 1 to this study, we provide a listing of some of the Darpa Dark Web software through the centre of 2016. The majority of the programs were a part of DARPA's attempt to create a Google-type search system of Dark Web content.

The Memex Project was in its third year in 2016, and detailed information regarding the program isn't generally available, the data which is available on the Surface Web is fragmentary.

A Few of the apps from the 2016 Darpa directory includes Dossier Stack, Formasaurus and HSProbe.

Dossier Stack is smart software delivered in the form of a library. A program taps into the library to perform certain entity-centric operations. Entities can include people, places, names of businesses, aliases, and other vital signifiers. The Dossier Stack enables a programmer to construct active search applications. These can learn what users need by monitoring and capturing their actions. The developer's commercial software makes it possible to mine vast flows of information and connect entities utilizing probabilistic inference algorithms. The programmer is Diffeo, a startup founded in 2012 that draws on experience from MIT and MetaCarta founder John Frank.84One area of interest for the firm is scraping the Web and creating knowledge graphs for unique entities. The idea is to refine in a more educated way the relationships among people, places, organizations, and named things. Diffeo integrates Basis Tech's language tools and uses SAP's in-memory database technology.

Formasaurus is a software component which provides information about form on a Web page. The python package decides whether the way is log-in, search box, registration, password recovery, mailing list, or a contact form. The system uses machine learning, so the precision of this component output increases over time. Hyperion Gray is the programmer of additional Memex modules, including Frontera (a Web-crawl prioritization routine) and Scrapy-Docker hub, apart for managing indexing program.

Tor Hidden Service Prober HSProbe is a multithreaded python application. The software makes use of Stem, a python controller library for Tor. Stem allows the program to use Tor's control protocol to script against the Tor process or build components which can determine the status of Tor hidden services and extract hidden support material. HSProbe was designed to make use of protocol error codes to decide what action to take when a covered service isn't reached. HSProbe tests whether specified Tor secret services (Onion addresses) are listening on one of a range of pre-specified ports.

Additionally, the program ascertains when the secret services are communicating over other protocols. The programmer/user provides a list of Onion addresses to be probed, and HSProbe outputs a list of results. Because the Dark Web offers encryption, it's perceived by Tor users to provide more anonymity than the Surface Web. Encryption can be broken.

With significant computing resources, most researchers will find that encryption with 256, 512, or 1024 bit keys aren't breakable. When faster or more advanced computers are available, speedy decryption may become the norm.

At this moment, an investigative team asking computer scientists to crack Dark Web encryption might be not able to read individual messages or transaction data.

Other tools worth mention are FinFisher, DaVinci and Galileo, Canvas, and Pegasus.

The FinFisher tools perform remote monitoring and remote access management. In a nutshell, the FinFisher malware is installed on a target's computer through an exploit; for example, the target downloads a Microsoft Word file that contains FinFisher code.

A goal may fall prey to an Adobe Flash exploit or an e-mail file with an attachment containing the FinFisher payload. Fin-Fisher can also masquerade as legitimate software, such as Firefox.

Essential functions include lawful interception and monitoring, Internet monitoring, blocking, information technology intrusion, satellite tracking, mobile tracking and location, passive tracking of landlines, SMS interception, speech recognition, link analysis, and radio frequency tracking, amongst others. Licensees of FinFisher tools include Britain, Qatar, United Arab Emirates, and America.

Company Hacking Team grows DaVinci and Galileo. Hacking Team's applications, according to some reports, is utilized by the US Federal Bureau of Investigations. Hacking Team's rootkit installs the Galileo remote control system (RCS).

The malware can be fixed if the investigator has access to a person of curiosity's computer when a suspected bad actor crosses a boundary. HackingTeam's tool consists of code to boot into a shell program and insert the rootkit. Hacking Team's surveillance suite for political interception of digital information might be detectable by anti-virus programs, but when removed, the firmware component reinstalls the rootkit. The company's rootkit software is malware. The feature of the tool is to embed instructions in the computing device central input operating system or "Unified Extensible Firmware Interface" (UEFI). Hacking Team's software approach isn't eliminated when the computing device's hard drive is replaced, and a fresh operating system is installed.

Hacking Team's method pulls merely the code from the UEFI and reinstalls the surveillance module when the computing device is rebooted. Hacking Team's software works on computers produced by Acer, Dell,

Hewlett-Packard, Lenovo, and Toshiba, among others. 128 The software, once installed, can forward the data generated by the user, Webcams, and other applications. This information is then uploaded to servers for additional analysis.

Canvas provides tools to tackle some exploits supported by the frame. Government agencies can use the structure to develop solutions to severe problems. These range from identifying a weakness in servers suspected of hosting secret solutions to finding gaps in computing devices seized by investigators. The business also provides consulting and engineering services to non-profit, and government organizations.

In a 2008 white paper, Aitel identified many of those security problems which are making headlines today. The 2008 document also anticipated the Snowden document release, the hacking and subsequent distribution of Hacking Team's applications, the occurrence of issues that make breaches like those in the Office of Personnel Management possible, and the exponential growth of vulnerabilities. Canvas is a package of software that equips investigators with offensive ability. The Canvas framework is easy to use with an interface which makes the rich functionality of the applications accessible to an investigator. The Canvas approach is to provide the investigator with a graphical workspace. The Canvas framework allows new polymorphic techniques to be developed that require chip emulation. Advanced exploits become more accessible to create and maintain.

NSO Group is a unique company in the field of Internet security software solutions and security research (https://bloomberg.com/research/stocks/private/).

The company's Pegasus software attracted attention after rumors circulated that the FBI recruited NSO to hack an iPhone utilized by the San Bernadino terrorists. Pegasus can intercept data sent to and from the telephone; for example, Gmail, Facebook, WhatsApp, and Skype information, amongst others. The NSO approach is to rely on a streamlined architecture that uses mobile phone networks and the international Internet backbone. The authorized licensee of the NSO Pegasus system or NSO's engineers put up a Pegasus workstation. The workstation interacts with the secure Pegasus installation server.

The licensee or a third party puts content containing a "stub" in a document, video, form, or another sort of file. The bad actor downloads the "stub," and the Pegasus installation server places the difficult-to-detect exploit software on the bad actor's computing device. Once this step is done, the Pegasus server receives information uploaded by the poor actor's computing device. The Pegasus licensee can then interact with the knowledge and take advantage of the many tools which Pegasus includes; for instance, geo-location of the bad actor's device.

References

iPhone update: Who is the mystery company behind malware hack?. https://news.com.au/technology/online/hacking/everything-we-know-about-nso-group-the-cyberarms-dealer-responsible-for-the-iphone-hack/news-story/da572d1c0b69dfa4a0b7ae632ee1f4e7

Order ElcomSoft Password Recovery Bundle online. https://elcomsoft.com/purchase/buy.php?product=eprb&ref=infopage

CHAPTER 2

Conversations in Cyberspace

A Conversation with Greg Walton

A D.Phil. candidate at Oxford's new Centre for Doctoral Training in Cyber Security, Greg Walton has recently joined the OII for his main research project. In the past Greg has investigated complex adaptive threats targeting civil society networks, and has worked extensively with Tibetan NGOs in the field in South Asia. Greg coordinated the primary field-based research for the GhostNet and the ShadowNet investigations in the Dalai Lama's Office and the Tibetan Government-in-Exile in Dharamsala, India, where he worked with a team that uncovered global cyber espionage botnets operating out of China, and penetrating the United Nations, NATO, governments, diplomatic missions, and civil society computers all over the world. Greg is a Fellow at the SecDev Foundation, having formerly been the SecDev Fellow at the Citizen Lab based at the Munk Centre, University of Toronto, and is a graduate of the Department of Peace Studies, University of Bradford (International Relations and Security Studies).

During May 2018 I had the chance to meet Gregory at Trinity College campus in Dublin, Ireland. We had a brief chat about the current state of Tibetan NGO, Dharamsala and the ShadowNet investigations. Here, is the transcript of the conversation we kept over e-mail during the month following our meeting in Dublin.

Q. You are researching malware in Central Asian NGOs with the SecDev Foundation, can you tell me a bit about SecDev and provide an overview of the "CyberSAR" project?

A. The SecDev Foundation is a not-for-profit "think-do tank" that works to promote digital safety and opportunity for civil society globally.

The Foundation directly executes programming in support of CSOs, women, youth and vulnerable groups in Eurasia, Middle East and North Africa, and Southeast Asia.

The CyberSAR project is one of these efforts. Interestingly, the technical research component of the CyberSAR project draws on cross-disciplinary methodologies first developed at the University of Cambridge by the Advanced Network Research Group. Founded just six months after the tragic events of 9/11, ANRG was a response to the demands to find an answer to the compelling need for new ways to address the instability and uncertainties that characterize the current climate of global insecurity.

The ANRG conducted research into the nexus between technical and social networks, and their consequences for global security, politics, finance, development, and conflict transformation. ANRG projects shared a common mixed methodology, which blended the use of technical methods for interrogating and mapping networks, while developing a proven expertise in contextual, in-field ethnography.

In 2006, the ANRG moved to Canada and became the SecDev Group, a digital risk consultancy. I worked with the SecDev Group at the Citizen Lab in 2008 where we uncovered a cyber espionage network operating out of a signals intelligence base in southern China that had infiltrated machines in the United Nations, NATO, government departments, diplomatic missions, and civil society computers around the world.

In 2011, SecDev Group co-founders Rafal Rohozinski and Deirdre Collings established the SecDev Foundation as an independent not-for-profit organization.

Q. … and the "CyberSAR project"?

A. Right…well, CyberSAR is typical of the Foundation's programming, and based on work in Syria, recently commended by the British Council (A new report from British Council and Build Up considers current peacetech initiatives responding to the Syrian crisis as well as options for future work using technology for peace building and development).

The research focused on three key areas:

1. Mapping existing peacetech responses to the Syrian crisis
2. Identifying key areas of British Council peacebuilding and development work where greater utilization of technology could enhance impact
3. Defining the different roles the British Council could play in this space and recommending a variety of strategies for future British Council investment in peace tech programmes.
4. CyberSAR is short for Cyber Security Assessment and Response project. CyberSAR is a multi-year effort that offers digital safety research and support for NGOs and media across the Eurasia region. CyberSAR strives to measurably reduce the cyber vulnerabilities of selected organizations through a combination of security assessments, real-time remediation of threats and risks to communication devices, extended training, and internal policy development. The CyberSAR project includes a research component that measures the efficacy of the intervention and seeks to understand and map the malware ecosystem in the post-Soviet space, that's where my work comes in.

Q. You are doing this research while you complete your PhD at Oxford?

A. Yes, one of the most innovative features of Oxford's Cyber Security CDT programme is the emphasis placed on working with industry partners to tackle real world cyber security problems.

From the first year onwards, I worked with organizations in industry and civil society such as iSIGHT Partners (subsequently acquired by FireEye), and the others on "wicked problems" in digital security, as diverse as tracking Advanced Persistent Threats from the PRC and Russia, predictive policing surveillance platforms in Xinjiang, Marxist complex systems engineering methodologies and governance in China.

Each of these engagements contributed to my understanding of the targeted digital threats civil society organizations face when they connect to the Internet, how they adapt to those threats, and provided quantitative and ethnographic data that informs my central DPhil thesis on the cyber security practices of NGOs: "Digital Insecurity in Context," based on a method that utilizes "big data" and "thick data."

Q. How do you detect malware incidents at these NGOs?

A. The CyberSAR project has deployed 20+ Zeropoint installations (a SaaS solutions that apply an intelligence-led approach and security heuristics to actively defend the enterprise against advanced cyber threats—including malware and ransomware—inside the perimeter, and out in the cloud) at NGOs in Central Asia, and is planning to deploy further instances at other NGOs and media entities in Caucasus and Eastern Europe.

Zeropoint is a SecDev Group-developed passive DNS system that detects digital threats including malware. Using DNS data Zeropoint can see active malware connections on the NGO's networks and halt its communication with its command and control infrastructure.

Q. Tell me more about your big data methods?

A. Well, using the data Zeropoint collects we are performing a quasi-experiment to measure the efficacy of the CyberSAR interventions using a robust methodology that applies time series analysis to DNS requests to track post-intervention digital behavioral change in a sample of the beneficiary organizations. At the suggestion of my main supervisor, and deputy director of the training centre at Oxford, Dr. Joss Wright, the methodology draws on best practices from epidemiology studies and public health interventions. The hypothesis underlying the experiment is that the CyberSAR intervention strengthens the overall digital security posture of the NGOs, as measured by number of malware attacks intercepted by Zeropoint, the cloud-based DNS firewall installed on the NGOs networks.

The research collects DNS requests from NGOs that are participating in the digital safety intervention, and compares a small treatment group of beneficiary organizations against DNS traffic from a second group in which the intervention has not yet taken place. Analysis of results will be based on a comparison interrupted time series (C/ITS) analysis of DNS traffic to measure the volume of detected anomalies associated with known or unknown cyber threat behaviors in the treatment and control groups. Interrupted time series (ITS) analysis is a "quasi- experimental" design with which to evaluate the longitudinal effects of interventions through regression modeling, where randomization is not an available option.

This project adds a control group to an ITS research design to produce a C/ITS analysis. This approach is important in real-world evaluations, as the quasi-experiment is taking place in a complex and dynamic socio-technical environment where a range of time-varying confounders will be either unmeasured or unknown. Furthermore, we use a multiple baseline design whereby the intervention happens at different field sites at different times.

Q. What results have you found?

A. Actually, the experiment is ongoing, with data collection underway at a number of Central Asian fieldsites.

Reports focusing on the experimental design of the project, and early findings from the process of designing and running the experiment, have been shared with trusted partners, and a paper submitted to an academic workshop focused on the cybersecurity of civil society organizations, where we highlight several challenges and considerations in designing and evaluating real-world cyber security interventions.

Q. You mentioned that you have borrowed methods from public health interventions. Is that an approach that you think has value for other cybersecurity problems?

A. The ITS study design is increasingly being used in epidemiology studies to evaluate the efficacy of public health interventions.

The turn toward analogical reasoning in contemporary academic cybersecurity discourse has seen the rise of modalities that challenge the logic of continuously prioritizing national security concerns in cyberspace, including seeing a global public health model being applied to digital safety, particularly when the focus is on mitigating unsafe user behavior that puts other users in their community at risk.

The epidemiology paradigm is also prevalent in the cybersecurity literature that deals with the theory of malware ecosystems, while a notable example of the practical application of a public health model by civil society organizations in response to systemic targeted malware attacks can be seen at another one of my field sites in the Tibetan exile diaspora.

Q. Your research focuses on DNS as the best place to stop malware for this case study, why is that?

A. The CyberSAR intervention, like many digital safety projects in the civil society sector, operates with constrained resources, and focusing on detecting malicious DNS traffic, is seen as among the more cost-effective technical interventions.

The Domain Name Service (DNS) is a foundational substrate of the global Internet, the lowest layer of the Internet, with the exception of the routing protocols themselves, and the most pervasive protocol. Malicious actors use DNS to propagate networks of compromised machines, such as botnets.

A recent survey by Cisco showed that 91.3 percent of malware uses DNS in attacks, either to receive instructions from Command and Control (C2) servers or for data exfiltration.

The same survey indicated that 67 percent of organizations do not monitor recursive (passive) DNS to detect anomalies associated with known or unknown cyber threat behaviors. Increasingly, however, network defenders are monitoring DNS traffic and applying static blacklists of malicious domains to block communications with botnets.

Q. Can you characterize the sort of malware families you are detecting in Central Asia?

A. We had hypothesized, prior to the experiment's pilot installations and initial site visits, that high-profile NGOs and independent media in Central Asia are specifically targeted online by other actors by dint of their professional activities. Our initial threat model referenced a growing literature on targeted digital threats to civil society actors.

Over the past decade, NGOs have become targets of spear phishing or social malware attacks, and have found it difficult to mitigate these threats.

In contrast to their under-resourced targets, the adversaries are often well-resourced and well-trained. Documented attacks on NGOs have often revealed a relatively high level of sophistication when the overall complexity of the attack is considered, particularly in the social engineering methods used, if not always in the code itself. In light of this observation Seth Hardy has proposed a metric that attempts to quantify the relative complexity of both the social engineering and the malicious code employed in a targeted malware attack.

It is argued that such a Targeted Threat Index (TTI) is a superior heuristic for assessing the sophistication of a threat—in comparison to technical analysis in isolation of the social context. A significant consequence of research analyzing targeted digital threats as socio-technical systems has been an increase in donor resources to modify user behavior among targeted populations through training programs, rather than on relying on strategies that over-emphasize technical risk mitigation through the deployment of software or hardware.

A significant motivation for the deployment of the DNS firewall was to mitigate the risk of targeted malware attacks by identifying the malicious domains associated with C2 infrastructure and blocking those domains. If one NGO in the research population was targeted, all the NGOs would be protected from that malicious infrastructure. This approach has worked to great effect in the Tibetan diaspora.

The digital security environment that we have observed so far, however, suggests that NGOs in the Central Asian region are more likely to be exposed to commodity threats, such as browser-based crypto jacking than to APTs.

Q. You work with NGOs or non-profit organizations for the most part. Are there significant differences between cybersecurity practices in the third sector as opposed to the corporate or government sectors?

A. Yes, NGOs often operate in challenging environments with constrained resources. Donors expect that beneficiaries will manage projects that are sustainable beyond a given funding cycle, and will have visible impact.

The participants of the CyberSAR experiment are typical of small scale civil society organization I am researching at other field sites, notably in Dharamsala, India, and Hong Kong, in that they face a wide range of cyber security threats that they are often ill-equipped to defend against.

The lack of both technical resources and training leaves many organizations vulnerable to even basic Internet mediated attacks. Breaches can have serious consequences for high risk, low capacity civil society organizations.

The exfiltration of confidential data introduces extreme risk into an already challenging operational environment. For example, outside the Central Asian region there are cases where staff members of compromised organizations have been detained, interrogated, and torture a direct consequence of a data breach.

Furthermore, the loss of confidential data can have effects beyond the compromised organization, leading to cascading effects throughout the donor-beneficiary ecosystem. It may be ironic, but the very same computer-mediated communications systems and information sharing practices that have been shown to empower civil society networks are increasingly channeling significant cyber risk.

At the same time, our field researchers' assessment at the sites in Central Asia, is that digital security behavior issues are prevalent, and that poor digital hygiene is a more significant organizational risk factor than APTs or other targeted campaigns.

With the applied research dimension of the CyberSAR project we aim to test this hypothesis, and quantify the impact that the improvement of digital hygiene through training has on the cybersecurity preparedness of an organization.

Q. Can we turn now to Chinese cyber espionage, particularly current APT campaigns targeting Tibetans?

Galaxy9

A Conversation with DeadWarrior420

Q. I have recently had a quick exchange of e-mails with Joseph Cox (Journalist, VICE and Motherboard Contributor) on the nature of Deep Web, Dark Net and also and law enforcement tracking measures. What are your observations on the following definitions?

> *The deep web is all content that is not indexed by search engines; so closed databases, e-mail inboxes, whatever it may be. The dark web is the small, almost tiny, collection of sites and services hosted via anonymity networks, such as Tor.*

A. I agree with Joseph definition. The deep web is its web pages that are not indexed by search engines. So when you go to Google, and you type in a search query, all the usual websites pop up or have the ability to pop up in that organic search. You know, if you are searching for whatever it is a Web site might pop up there with the deep web is the deep web is all of the web pages that are out there on the Internet that for whatever reason are not indexed by the search engine. So, if you searched they would not show up in Google, they would not show up and be they would not show up on Yahoo or AltaVista or whatever else. That is all the deep web is the deep web are the web pages that are not indexed by search engines.

Search engines index all web pages. So what are they trying to hide that circumstances do not index them? Well in the modern era you know 2013 and so forth. Many Web pages are not indexed by search engines such as Google and Yahoo. Because they are behind login walls.

If you go to a site, let's say you go to a WordPress site or you go to some community Web site, and you have to login. The only way to be able to access the content on that Web site is if you can log in. Now all of us circle engines they have these little algorithms that run around and they are called either spiders or robots. These spiders or robots go out, and they navigate the Web. So, basically they kind of just let them loose. Also, what happens is these spiders and robots they go out they catalogue all the Web pages that they can find.

They catalogue all the Web pages that are linked to by other web pages. Also, then they follow that and go along go and grab information and index all of these different Web pages that are out there. Well, their issue is to imagine they are going along with their index an index an index an index. Moreover, they are about to index a Web site. However, when they get to the Web site, it asks for a username a password.

Well, that robot cannot get passed because of not a real user, so it does not have a username and password. So websites much of Web sites such as Facebook are considered deep web directly because Google does not index them. There's a substantial massive argument going on right now where Google says that they should be able to index more Facebook and Facebook allows them to access a whole big thing.

However, but what you should understand is that there are just many pages within Facebook that cannot be indexed by Google or being or anybody else. Therefore that would be considered the deep web. If you set up a community site and let's say you close it off, so it is it is private, only private members can access the information. So you set up a bulletin board, but then you do not want this to be public you only want you to know your fellow users to be able to access it.

The same thing would be right when one of these spiders a robot from Google or Yahoo go to a to scan your web pages. They will be blocked by the username and password that's the first reason why there is a lot of deep web pages out there you need login credentials. That is the other reason that there are deep web pages is you can ask through coding for these search engines to not index your web page for whatever reason. So there's something called the robots dot text file. You put that into the root of your Web site. So basically the same place where your index that a T.M. or a mail or whatever it is if you put in what's called a robot is not text file within that file you can ask these search engines not to index you.

You know a lot of us a lot of us are not overly worried about putting information out onto the Internet, but we do not want to overdo it. Right. So let's say you have a club or you have an organization and you want to be able to put on to the Web. Let's say the board members names. If other members need to get in contact with somebody or if somebody else needs to see a listing of who the board members are you want to be output that on the Web. So it is one of those things that you know you do not care if the public sees it, on the other hand, you do not necessarily want this thing showing up in a Google search. You know, if somebody goes to the Web page if somebody knows what the Web pages.

That is fine if they see it.

If they do not know what the web page is, you do not want them to know about it. Well, then that is what you might put into robots that text file to state that you do not want the search engines to index the pages because again you do not want it to show up in Google or Yahoo or being so on and so forth.

Again this is not nefarious. This is not cool. This is not sexy. This may be the membership roster for your local Elks Club or Rotary Club or something like that again fundamentally we do not care if it is public you prefer it be just not completely and utterly out there. So robots, not x files were used for a long time. When you go back to websites that were built like 10 years ago lots of people were putting up Web pages, and they did not want them to be indexed by the likes of Google, and so they use these robots dot TX file. Now the critical thing to understand about the robots that 65 is it is only a suggestion for the web crawlers. So the spiders and the robots that Google and Yahoo and all that send out there when they go to your Web site they will look for robotics. If they read the robots that text file it tells them what you would prefer that you prefer that the site not is indexed, but they can go ahead and indexed it regardless.

This is not like when you use a robot start 65. This is not like a mandatory federal law or something it is just kind of like a nicety. So those are the main reasons that we get what's called the deep web, so these are the Websites that are not indexed by Google Yahoo. Any of these search engines.

Moreover, again it is generally because either there's some logging credential or there are the robots start next fall. So let's go over to the computer for a second. Yes so you can see a couple of things, and maybe this will get a little bit clearer for you. So I just brought up this Web page here.

If you go to robots .txt you can get a lot more information about the robots, not a text file. So basically again all of these files you can create this in notepad.

It is not a female, and it is not anything like that is just robots that Eccky all you do is you put in this user agent Colan star disallow coal and slash. Also, basically what that says is it says to all those crawlers and robot please do not index this website. Moreover, that is all you have to do. Also, then you to have a Website on the deep web. Not only that but even on things like Wordpress. So my clearnet blog is built on WordPress. If you go in here you will see if you go down to setting's reading there's a little checkbox search engine visibility you can discourage search engines from indexing this site. Again it is up to the search engines to honor this request, but generally they do so if I check off this box it will tell the search engines please do not index the site so even though it is a full site even though it is a big site. All of that basically will drop off of Google and Yahoo and being so on and so forth. That is all you do to create the deep web that's all there is to the right.

I do not know why people think it is impressive and fresh and fancy again. I think it is I think it is merely one of those we have gotten so used to being able to use search engines to find anything on the Internet. It seems that if you cannot use a search engine to find information, then it must be again cool or nefarious or something like that.

The reality is you know many times again. There's login credential that blocks robots from Serkin. There are a robot start X Files that block or that try to block search engines from indexing, and there's also really crappy code again when you are thinking about the Internet. Many you folks many you folks were not even born when the Internet you know popped out in 1992. Well you may not realize is that there are many Websites still up and running that got coded a long, long, long time ago when we were all still trying to figure out what the hell we were supposed to be doing.

Some of these in deep web websites are just Web sites that were coded so horribly that even the robots do not know what to do with them. You know what I am saying. However, that is all the deep web the deep web is simply web pages that are not indexed by Google or any of the other search engines for whatever reason.

Q. Deep Web and Dark Net? What is the difference?

A. The deep web is a specific concept. The dark net is a specific concept Tor or Freenet are specific products or services. These are all different things that vaguely encompass the same realm. So this is something that's very important for you to understand. So when we talked about in the introduction to the deep web class the deep web is any web page that is not indexed by a search engine for whatever reason whether it's the robots start t file tells a certain kind of bugger off that you don't want the Web site to be indexed whether the Web site is some kind of content management system where it requires a login username credentials to get past the initial screen. Therefore the little Google spiders can't get past or if it's part of something called a dark net. When we're talking about a dark net basically this is a cluster of computers that are meshed together in order to create a network and in order to be able to access those computers or those services you have to have special software installed onto your computer. If basically these web services that are out there Google cannot simply be able to go out or Yahoo can't simply go be able to go out and index because you have to have some type of software on your computer. So, the dark net is a very specific concept within the larger idea of the deep web. So when we're talking about the dark darknet basically we're talking about one of two products although there are other options out there. Generally we are talking about Tor. And more importantly or more specifically Tor services.

There's also something called Freenet which allows you to do the same thing that we're going to be talking about today. Basically those are the services that encompass the dark net is considered so many times when people are talking about the darknet they are in fact talking about poor services. They use those words interchangeably when in fact they're not. Tor services are a specific product.

The Dark Net itself is more of a concept an idea. So we're talking about the darknet the essential definition of a darknet is in order to access the darknet. You have to have some kind of special software installed onto your computer so the darknet anything that comprises a darknet it has to use the TCAP IP protocols it has to be theoretically Internet accessible but you have to do something special in order to get into it. So the first thing is although it uses Internet technologies to maintain itself and to do the communication you have that you have to add something else in order to be able to access the information within that Darknet.

The other main concept with darkness is that it's supposed to try to maintain your anonymity. So when you go on there it's supposed to try to maintain your ability to stay anonymous. So in normal IP traffic in normal network traffic nobody cares about whether or not you're anonymous you may care but the original the original creators of TCAP the original creators of the Internet didn't care. The more communication that goes back and forth the better for them. So when we're talking about TCAP IP packets TCAP IP headers.

What's important to understand there is that contains a lot of identifiable information that basically points back to you. So if anybody gets a hold of that packet they can gather information and be able to track back to you. Well in the modern world you know the modern world of anonymous people want to keep their anonymity so they don't want to be tracked back.

The big concept with the darknet is when you go onto the darknet when you use a darknet that you should be able to maintain your anonymity. So, the important part is it uses normal Internet and IP and all that technology you have to install software in order to be able to access it. And it's a to maintain your anonymity. And again this can be done in multiple ways. There are multiple different products out there in order to create Darknet. Again the most popular is something called TOR. And again there's also Freenet which is a lot of people additionally use. Now when you're talking about Tor basically the initial idea for Tor was that you would be able to Rã your data traffic through multiple different computers that are all connected into this Tor network. So that you could bypass filters in your country so if you were in an autocratic country where they didn't want you to be able to watch CNN dot com or the Daily Show you would be able to be able to connect to the TOR network and it would rout your communication through a hundred or however many computers to get the so that you can access networks outside of what's being blocked. Also by routing information through this massive network it would keep your anonymity. So if you go to CNN dot com or if you go to a Web site the information that that Website will be able to glean from you would not be personally identifiable it would be part of this whole mesh of the TOR. So the original idea with TOR is it was supposed to keep your anonymity for going to normal websites if you were going to CNN back home if you were going to Bank of America dot com if you were going to Wikipedia if you were going to Anonymous We love anonymous dot com. You know if you try to go to those sites the original idea was it keeps your anonymity there. Well then they came up with the idea of something called Tor services. Now it's very important to understand that when we're talking about Web sites actually within Tor itself these are called Tor services. So what they decided what they came up with is instead of always routing all the all the traffic out to Web sites in the normal Internet that you would be able to create and host Websites on your own computers at home and then through the power of Tor people would simply be able to be redirected to you. So basically you can use a web browser you can connect to Tor and then you could use a services address to go to this specific Web site that you want to go to. Now, why this is powerful is because since you're in the Tor network and everything tries to maintain your anonymity even the web servers themselves maintain the anonymity.

If you're trying to do a black market website if you're trying to sell crack if you're trying to create the next Wikipedia you can actually set up a Website that the entire world can get to. But the system itself that writes the information to that Website. We'll try to maintain your anonymity. So that is why this is very powerful so when people are talking about the darknet this is what they're talking about they're talking about these Tor services or the services that you can also get by using Freenet so these are Web sites but they are all within the Tor cloud. So you can't go to Google and go like black market dot com and get to one of these sites. Basically you have to have the Tor software installed on your computer then you can open the browser then you can go to one of these services addresses and that will drop you onto the site once you're dropped onto the site. We are then now talking about standard web-based technologies.

ASTM Ellan javascript HP whatever is a standard web server. It is simply connected to the Internet using one of these services. So let's go to the computer for a second so I can show you a couple of things just to give you a better idea of how all of this stuff kind of works.

So basically again whenever we are talking about the darknet the two things that we are going to be talking about is either Tor so that you can find Tor at Tor Project dot or Freenet. So again share chat browse anonymously on the free network. Again these create their networks within the Internet. Now, what have I been showing you today? If you go down, there's a lot of different things you can download and use with your board. I downloaded news today is something called the Tor browser. So instead of installing the full suite onto my computer, this is just a web browser that you can install on your computer and use the Tor network. Once I installed the Tor browser as we can see here this is Tor browser. It is just a Firefox derivative, and I have come to one of the directories they have in store. So, this is one of the top directories. What you will see is this is the eServices address up here. Also, you will notice it looks absolutely and utterly nothing like a standard DNS address that you are used to. You know ... boot info no. Whenever you set up your Web server on to Tor and ask and connect the services they will automatically give you one of these services addresses, so you do not get to say what it is and it will be a whole mess. Yes, it is. Remember when you are going to be using these two services you are not going to get the first human-readable addresses. With a lot of these things once you find them bookmark the hell out of them because I do not know about you but I am not going to be a remember them. Now if you go down. Primarily this works like any other web browser, but it is all within these services. So I clicked on this little black market link over here, and if we open this up, we can see this is a different services address and as for this Black Market Reloaded I am not going to log into any of this stuff because I do not.

I do not want to be on the NSA radar. But this is the basic idea behind the darknet. So when I am going to these Websites, this is trying to maintain my anonymity. So also I cannot find any information out about the web servers unless I try to hack them myself. So generally if we were on the usual web, I could do.

Who is sir?

Sure I could do many ways to try to find out who runs this Website or where the server is located again within the darknet within Tor. That functionality is not there. However, that is that is all there is.

For the most part the darkness. So the darknet is merely a network of computers on the Internet that uses standard Internet-type technology that is meshed together.

You have to use a particular piece of software tool in order to access them. Moreover, they try to maintain your anonymity. That is what the darkness sometimes is a tor service sometimes as a Freenet sometimes there are a lot of other pieces of software there's a lot of other specific services out there. The idea behind the darknet is that this overall methodology anonymity separated service using standard Internet type technologies and that is that is the darknet for you. We are going to be doing more classes on Tor services and some other things, but I figured this would be a way to clear some things up so that darknet is a component of the deep web, Tor.

Is something that uses the darknet ideology primarily but these are all entirely separate things. Also, so you should keep keeping that in mind whenever going to be dealing with this stuff. So as you know I am Eli, the computer guy. Today's class was an introduction to the darknet. As always I enjoyed teaching this class and look forward to the next one.

Q. From your experience in the Anonymous group/movement, do you think it is possible to be fully anonymous online?

A. Think about this: the average human has about 30,000 thoughts a day, most of them are repetitions. Most of those thoughts are external programming, not internal thoughts. Due to information overload, many of us find it hard to form our own thoughts, let alone think freely. Brain overload causes a passive state, you become tired and too weak to be aware. Unawareness eventually leads to being easily controlled and manipulated.

If you knew all this, would you care more about hiding your location or preserving the privacy of your thoughts?

You know the whole idea of staying anonymous online is ridiculous and foolish and just idiotic like the thought that you would use any services on the Internet and the web and be anonymous is a joke. It is laughable. It is beyond laughable. It is something that that should be scoffed at. It just doesn't. It's the foolishness that people who watch movies and then think they're hackers come up with right.

There is no real way to stay anonymous online. Only your data can be anonymous, not you. Yes, you can make the life of governments harder by sending your location across the globe, yet, if necessary, they will find you using a combination of tools, techniques and skills that are unique and unachievable even by the best hackers in the world. The reality is that you can always be tracked online. The only question is how many resources does the person who wants to track you want to devote to trying to track you. So even if you even if you know to do this whole hacker thing in your ear you are bouncing your packets through multiple proxy servers MVP ends and Tor network and all this kind of horse crap.

One your internets your actual Internet connection speed is going to go back go back down to like two kilobits per second. But to even if you do that even if you balance your or your Internet traffic through 10 different proxy servers let's just say it still works. You can still be tracked. The reality is the reality is that when the Internet was developed when TCAP before the Internet Protocol. The networking protocol that we use for the Internet was developed. They weren't worried about being anonymous. This was all supposed to be trusted computers on trusted networks communicating with each other. And why would you want to be anonymous if it's trusted computers on trusted networks talking to other trusted computers on other trusted networks it just been anonymous just did not come up or at least was not put into the plan when the whole Internet and the world wide web as it's been developed now was being created.

Beyond that there's a lot of commercial interests and also government interests out there to be able to track people when they go online. And so the issue is basically what you have when you go in when you go on the Internet you have to realize is one this system was never Arfeen built for you to be anonymous and to lots of lots of companies a lot of government organization with billions of dollars and budgets have no interest in you staying anonymous. So it's like you know cracking your privacy online. Yeah. Yeah you're just not anonymous online. Yeah. Yeah I don't I don't even know why people ask. It's funny. Like I know I kind of was a smart ass and I'm like snarky when I say this but I really want you guys to understand why is it good. It is laughable. The idea that you would have privacy or that things would be anonymous online is so it is it is laughable it is just like that's funny. Right.

So no you can't be.

You can't be 100 percent anonymous online even if you use VPN servers are not going to be necessarily anonymous even if you use proxy servers you're not going to be anonymous. Even the Tor network you know the FBI just took down a whole bunch of tourist sites and cracked down on Tor users because they were able to crack the Tor network. And that's what you that's what you just have to realize is that there's just so many ways to screw with you when you go online that there's just there's almost no way to be anonymous.

When you go online would be to steal somebody else's computer take it to a random coffee shop use the Internet for maybe five minutes, take the computer to throw it in the trash and walk away and make sure you use gloves your fingerprints on it and that might work maybe. Probably not because you guys don't even really like. It is so cool.

All the stuff that is out there to track those logs is incredible. You have even heard of. It is called biometrics. So when you think about biometrics, you think about things like fingerprint scanners and eyeball scanners and face scanners and all that.

However, there's another thing called biometrics that identifies you based on how you use your computer. So when you when you do something like You go to a Web site and you plug in a search term so you search for something on the Internet they can determine who you are by how long it takes you to type in Q, W, E, and so on. When you type in that search query, it will determine who you are based on how long you pressed down an individual key for. So when you press T that you press down on t four point zero three milliseconds and when you press down one you press down and four point zero five milliseconds. So when you type out a whole world that that takes that takes one point one five seconds or whatever like that.

Moreover, they can take all of that information and assign that a number and that number is now you. Also, now that they have a number they can track other things you know geolocation and all that kind of stuff. It is awesome. Privacy does not like you know I like it. Again I do not want to talk to you guys about this stuff. It is not about ethics. It is not about morals. I am not going into what's right or wrong I am all that kind of stuff we are just we are just taking that off the table we are just talking about what it is now. Moreover, let me tell you the concept of privacy and anonymity online is it is it is utterly laughable.

I would not worry about it if you want to be entirely anonymous online. Give up give it up. Because again I say with like that biometric thing they cannot even track you so if you went to a library to log in to the Websites and do whatever you are doing they could track that.

Also, then there's some exciting stuff where you know you get enough people's patterns for how they do things and people in different areas of the world do things very particularly even within particular neighborhoods. So if you can figure out things like the EU biometrics and behavior patterns, and you know somebody at the library has these particular behavior patterns, and we know because we've done previous research that this particular neighborhood the people in that neighborhood are likely to have the same behavior patterns, even if you're going to a public library, they can still in that way track you back to where you've come from …

It is not I do not know where people come up with the whole idea. I want to be anonymous online.

It is a good dream but doesn't exist. So again, there's no way to stifle an anonymous online system. Functionally is not built for you to stay anonymous and all the people with any power do not want you to stay anonymous. So there you go. Having anonymity online is a fantasy. Protect your data, focus on encryption, there is no future in hiding your location.

Q. Interesting, what about VPNs?

A. Consumer virtual private networks are terrible. That is at least this privacy is your primary concern. There are of course different threat models which will vary for each person. But as a general rule most VPN are just Kamm's system your browsing data. Sometimes they even make you pay for it. But there is an issue at the user side when it comes to privacy and even the trusted ones when you visit a Website over a VPN. The only thing that changes on your advertising profile they maintain is your IP address. Websites will still be able to track your browsing history and identify you through your browsing habits.

The only people you are protecting your browsing history from are your Internet service provider and that's only assuming you have a proper VPN that doesn't leave your private information to anyone. To understand why this is a case you need to learn three things. What is a virtual private network. Hovey means work and how websites track you to answer the first question we're going to look at the purpose. Why virtual private networks enter the market as Internet was becoming predominantly widespread means of communication. Companies started building local networks to speed up their business.

However, as businesses grew in size many of them started to spread to offsite locations and centre employees to work from home or while travelling to connect to a company local area networks at a reasonable distance. Business would have to dedicate a real world connection through physical infrastructure such as leased lines. This wasn't a problem if a company had to shorter distance networks to bridge the longer distance and the more Networks a company needed. The cost of lease lines would grow exponentially. Internet is a public network open and visible to everyone. No company could afford to use the open Internet and risk data breaches and have their private information stolen by anyone. They needed a secure connection. That was fast reliable and cost effective.

Thus can Virtual Private Networks a VPN is a private network that makes a virtual connection through a public network which could easily be and in most cases even worse. The Internet connection through a VPN could answer a specific company needs like speed data integrity or confidentiality. Virtual Private Network is a flexible model that can adapt to various standards. Corporations needed to adopt. This is the first very important point. There is no single standard for building a VPN. Each provider has its own structure and protocols which offer different features and not all of them are privacy. So how do VPN work. Basically what a VPN does is that it takes packets of data that will typically run through an insecure network like Internet encapsulates them in an entirely new packet and puts its VPN header on top of it. In the source of information this process is called startling, and it is how VPN has your initial IP

CONVERSATIONS IN CYBERSPACE   41

address. This is why you can trigger upsized to have a different IP and bypass geolocation censorship. But this is not what guarantees the confidentiality of your data. For that you need encryption data. Confidentiality was the most critical feature. Companies usually needed and achieve that by encrypting the traffic between a client and the VPN server. This means that a company VPN client can encrypt data coming from their employee's laptop working out in the field and connected to our local Wifi companies. This is a near perfect security because they can choose to host the VPN server as their own headquarters where the VPN decrypts all the traffic encryption doesn't necessarily mean privacy for companies encrypting their network to give them security layer to guard their data from outside adversaries. But it didn't give their employees within their network any level of privacy because the leadership of the company had direct access to every server and desktop traffic of everyone connected to that VPN through a consumer VPN. You don't VPN server you have to trust a company maintaining the VPN server with your data encryption still takes place on your device where their VPN clan configures your computers connection to be trusted and encrypted through the VPN. When the VPN server receives your data it decrypts it and sends the request to a Web site.

You are trying to visit purely from analyzing the IP address. The website will only see the connection from a private VPN server and not yours provided it's a good VPN that doesn't leak other data. Can identify you. So by design, this is an entirely different model from end to end encryption. In e-mail communication and you shoot adjust your expectations accordingly.

The reason why a VPN works to protect corporate privacy but fail at guarding consumer privacy is the fundamental design of VPN technology VPN server is always going to know someone personally identifiable information about you whether it's a real IP address information you submitted upon account creation and information taken from their payment method. The process of collecting this information is called, and it is not much you can do to verify what the company does with user locks to help you better understand that issue with privacy on VPN. We're going to compare end to end encrypted e-mail service and VPN service provided by the same company.

Proton mails end to end encryption is done so well that if you lose your password, they are only able to recover access to your account.

However, all their messages will be discarded forever. You lose your decryption key. This may come as an inconvenience, but it is an excellent defence mechanism to protect yourself from hackers. Nobody not even Protonmail can get access to her messages for the same company that offers Protonmail also offers Proton VPN and your expectations for the privacy of these two products shows to differ significantly with e-mail encryption Protonmail can block itself from accessing your messages quickly.

Users generated decryption keys and printed e-mail exchanges encryption keys, and mail doesn't decrypt your message. Your web browser does. However, Proton VPN has to both encrypt and decrypt your information making a program VPN server a single point of failure significant cybersecurity no. Disclaimer This is not just about Proton VPN every VPN provider has this problem. It's technologically impossible to create a consumer VPN with perfect privacy. Our VPN is useless for general Internet consumers for a vast majority of opinions out there. Yes, but for the trusted few and for specific threat models, Philippines can offer some protection from your ISP advertisers and non state hackers. For example, the United States Federal Communications Commission recently repealed a rule barring ISP from so your browsing history for advertising purposes. This is an incredible invasion of privacy because they record what do you do in your living room to money political, economic activity. So if you are in the United States, its fees are your browsing history to whomever they want.

This is not just a privacy validation but also a security risk because they're selling your private information over the Internet and once they sell your browsing habits checkers and foreign governments can and indeed do intercept those exchanges to steal a copy of her private life. There are databases of private information on millions of people available for sale or for free. So you'll never know it is until we become a victim of cybercrime.

Your security is in your hands. Only. Provided you can find a trusted VPN server. However, be aware we are talking about a great deal of trust here. Having your browsing habits from your ISP is sensible. However, the way the Internet works you always have to trust someone and you need to decide for yourself whether it's going to be your monopolistic Internet service provider giving your data caps. Internet censorship and overpriced, slow broadband or a virtual private network operated by privacy activists.

So, how do you choose the VPN provider?

Well, you need to do two things you need to evaluate your friend model. We will go over that on my channel in the future, and you'll need to do much research and educate yourself about a topic.

Never trust a single source.

Don't even look at Torrent Freak or peacemaker reviews. Look at what the community is saying about VPN providers. One good source of reviews of many features from many VPN providers is that one privacy site dot net Reddit is an excellent source of customer reviews and you can browse those without having it ready to count. You need to ask yourself some questions to see what you care about the most. First, the jurisdiction of the VPN provider is it in any of the 14 ays countries that collaborate with the NSA on mass surveillance. Their government could force the log users what steps are you willing to take against government's surveillance.

Do you want to keep your private information away from manipulative advertisers?

Are you looking for protection of your sensitive information from heteros and cybercriminals?

Mostly when you are on a public Wi-Fi is there a goal bypassing government censorship and geolocation of Internet content. What countries do you want to connect to websites from? How much are you willing to pay for a VPN. All of these questions are part of analyzing your threat model. If privacy is our biggest concern, then VPN is not the solution. Tories if you want better security when you connect to a Starbucks Wifi VPN is an excellent remedy. Never trust a free VPN. Those are the most Cammi out of all although VPN can't make it a cheaper solution for business networking compared to Willey's lanes. It's still pretty expensive to offer it as a free service. However, now we are getting to us for a third and most problematic question.

How can websites wreck you even if you use a VPN?

Let's say you find and buy your monthly subscription and renounce the VPN providers and then you do something like this. You've successfully configured your VPN connection. Then you open your favorite web browser which should never be chrome. However, statistically, it most likely will be you look into your Gmail which chrome takes us if you are looking into the browser itself for sinking, and then you browse the web for all kinds of purposes. Education work entertainment shopping travel and whatever else you just handed over all of your private information to the most pervasive violence corporation in the world. China doesn't have the surveillance capabilities of Google and Google will sell your privacy to every Web site and retailer you visit. Block trickers properly you're just wasting your money. You need to reassess your model. You need to ask yourself from whom are you trying to protect your private information.

Your Internet service provider vendors of software and applications connected to the Internet Web site operators, advertisers, governments and hackers all of your adversaries use common points of access for data collection over browsing history. Either for your ISP trickers on websites ID calls on software and applications and online communication tools like e-mails and instant messengers for Websites using tractors everything about your identity remains unchanged except for your IP address.

When he does a VPN what stays visible is the device which probably has a unique Eidi your hardware-software configuration operating system software versions, web browser plugins, extensions and screen resolution, the combination of all of this information and your writing habits make a unique personal identification. Moreover, what's more, you're giving many websites your real name to confirm your identity. Like your Facebook and e-mail accounts, and every online retailer that has your payment info.

If you're serious about privacy, you'll need to block all of these access points VPN. Black Eyed Peas Tor blocks governments. How do black Web sites from tracking you by using previously configured web browsers and by compartmentalizing your browsing habits of separate browsers? Several extensions look for accuracy at school keys and traffic with scripts. Among the best are your metrics. No script. Kubelik origin.

Privacy Badger cookie although delete and decentralize. You don't need to use all of these configured adequately to your metrics will make all the others redundant. Take Kubelik origin and privacy badger and search your browser to look. Third party cookies and delete them regularly. But even if you go all these links you'd still feel if you do the same mistake as I described earlier you have to block access to websites with your online accounts even pseudonymous ones to your browsing habits. Have a separate browser for your social media e-mail and banking and a separate browser for general surfing. Only if you will of old trackers. Only if he put a wall between your online identities and browsing habits. Only then using a trusted privacy focus on the VPN has some sense.

Q. Tell me about Tor

A. Tor is a service that you use to try to provide anonymity while you are on the Internet. Tor is a service that helps create what is called The Dark Net. Basically Internet networks that you can only access if you have special software installed on your computer. So not only does Tor allow you to surf the Internet anonymously but it allows you also anonymously to host websites. So, if you want to create a new Website for some dissident political organization something like that. You usually have to go out you have to register a domain name you have to buy a hosting account. If you on a country that's trying to crack down on things like that they can easily track you back to wherever you are. Well, with something called a secret service within Tor you can actually host websites and just as people's anonymity is kept for navigating through the web. This is also true for you when you are hosting the server. Nobody knows who you are or where that server resides. TOR was created some years ago by the U.S. Naval Research Laboratory so one of the ideas that they were having one of the things that they were trying to figure out how to secure the transport of information between two locations. Especially when they have soldiers or naval people out in the field, the question was how on open Internet connections could you communicate back with the Home Office without the information either being captured or something called traffic analysis being done.

Moreover, so they came up with TOR. So basically when you connect to the TOR system using your computer you're the traffic on the tour system is encrypted and when you connect out to a server in the outside world that server will not know where you are coming from. So, if you are trying to hide your location, it is relatively easy. Now basically how the law allows this to happen is it is necessarily a mesh of proxy servers secure proxy servers, so we had a class on proxy servers before mainly with a proxy server y0ou connect your computer to the proxy server and then from the proxy server you go out to the Internet. So let's say you are trying to bypass some firewall in your college's network. You connect to a proxy server, and then all of your information is relayed through that proxy server out to the Internet. So you can get to your BitTorrent or your Porin or whatever it is you are trying to get to. Well, the idea with TOR is that it's a mesh of these proxy servers. So instead of just going through one proxy server, you may go through 3 4 5 6 7 8 9 10 proxy servers. So let's go to the computer just for one second. Over to my little digital whiteboards, you can understand what we are talking about here.

So in order to keep your security the main issue that Tor is trying to deal with is if you are sitting at your computer here and you're trying to get to a server out here it's a www.CNN.com right. What's going to happen is you're gonna connect to the Internet. And then from there, you're going to go to the server. CNN dot com and your external IP addresses to 55 66 dots 1 when you connect the CNN dot com CNN dot com is going to be able to see what your external IP addresses.

Now we have talked about geolocation before with IP addresses and once somebody knows what your IP address is it is straightforward to locate where you are you are physically at. So the issue is not only can CNN dot com know what your external IP addresses but if somebody like the NSA or some intelligence agency is listening on the traffic they also know where you are coming from. So, the idea with TOR is. Instead of going just through the open Internet to CNN dot com. What happens is you go into the Tor network Tor has numerous relays so when you install Tor on your computer not only can you use the Tor network but also you can set up a relay a relay is basically like a proxy. So what happens is if you try to get the CNN dot com your connection goes to one tour relay and then it goes to another treeline and then it goes to another Trilla and then it goes to another Triola and then it goes out to CNN. I'm not sure exactly how many relays it goes through, but it goes through a number. The important thing with this isn't CNN dot com you know your address is 2 855 to 66 out one CNN dot com does not see you're externalizing putrescent it sees the external IP address of whatever the last relay is. So let's say 2 0 1 77. 20 to six. So basically this tries to high what your external IP addresses. So either the company can't go back and figure out who you are or get an NSA or any of these intelligence agencies can't do that.

That's essentially the idea of what's going on with TOR is it's a mesh of these proxy servers to try to protect your communication while it's in route. So with this, the one thing you have to understand is while your traffic is within that poor network that your mesh is encrypted but do be careful we will have a class on security and safety concerns with TOR your.

Traffic is not encrypted between you and the first relay you go to. And it's not encrypted between the final relay that the exit relay that you're coming out of. The Website or the service that you're going to so this is one thing that you have to be careful with. While it is in the network, it is encrypted, but otherwise, it's not. Now one of the questions you may have is well what about these individual relays can they try to track information and try to locate people within the network. Also, the exciting thing with TOR is that e relay only has information about the relays it is connected to. So let's say you go through five relays in order to get out the CNN dot com relay in there. It knows the upstream relay, and it knows the downstream relay, but it doesn't know anything beyond that. So that is one of the ways that they keep an eye on the enemy is that the relays only know the other relays that they are directly connected to. They don't know how traffic is being routed in the overall network.

With TOR primarily in order to keep the secure ease is with Rao through the right relays is stable for approximately 10 minutes. So basically when your computer connects into the Tor network it creates a route for you through these two relays, and you will keep that same account for approximately 10 minutes, and then after 10 minutes, it will drop and then you will see they will give you a different rule. Again this is a way in order to keep security on the network. Now when we talk about the darknet or when some people talk about the deep web we're talking about is something called Hidden services within Tor. So there are what are called dot onion sites. Right. These are Web sites that are hosted within TOR itself. So you can't do WWW something or other dot onion and go there. You have to have Tor properly installed on your computer.

You have to have Tor running, and then you can go to what is called Hidden services. Now with these hidden services they have a noxious Lely a horrible domain name. They are not what you would consider human readable. Mostly whenever you initialize a secret service on the TOR network what happens is they give you a random string of digits and letters dot onion. So whenever you are looking at these deep webs or these Tor sites these hidden services sites they will have really obnoxious names on them, and that is just one of the things they should consider. So when you're talking about these darknet sites or these dot onion sites these hidden services all this as these are Web sites that are hosted on the network again. The reason why that's so important is now whenever you bring up a web server, and you put it on Tor network nobody can know who it is that's actually brought up the servers so you could bring this up in the middle of Egypt and have it talking about the political party and you will also keep anonymity for that web server. So that's what the secret services are. So let's go over to the other computer for a second so that I can show you your Web site and you can get an idea of how you would go about using tours in the real world.

If you want to start using Tor, all you got to have to do is go to Tor Project dot org, and all the information and the downloads and everything is here. Now when we go down, Tor has many different products that you can use, and you should take a take a look at all of them. So, the main thing is that there is Tor itself so if we click on Tor and the download.

But and this is where you can download and install Tor onto your computer. So this is where you install it on your computer. Now the one thing they're gonna give you is they're going to give you a lot of warnings. Now it is essential that you understand Tor is one specific tool that is used to protect your privacy. You know with nefarious players out there on the Internet there are ways to bypass everything right. So they're going to tell you they're going to give you some warnings here.

Now some of the warnings that they give you is they ask you to use the Tor Browser I'll show you that in a second. So there's the first derivative of Firefox called the Tor browser that will try to keep your privacy for you. Then it also tells you don't enable or install browser plugins. So this is very important is because when you are on the Internet primarily with TOR it is trying to get going for your web browser it is going to protect you or your privacy it is going to try to protect your privacy. But within your web browser remember there's a lot of other programs that are running quicktime flash things like that Tor doesn't necessarily keep those individual plugins from giving away your private information. So you have to be careful that you use a TV version of Web sites. So basically this is Website encryption. Remember as I told you the eggs. The if the information is not encrypted between the exit relay and whatever Web site you're going to, so if NSA is going to try to grab your information they could try to grab it between exit relay and whatever site you're going to if you use a TDP s or if you use encryption. And that's one way to try to stop that.

Don't open documents downloaded through Tor while online.

I've shown you tricks using things like I frames where if you open up a document with things like eye frames or other stuff it will try to grab your information and send it and then use bridges or find a company we'll talk about that stuff later. So this is some information that you should keep in mind when you were going to be using Tor. Again with all the security things we've got to think about those there's a specific product is a specific service to protect you in one way. But don't assume it will completely protect you from everything. So you can either download Tor, or you can go and here they have something called tails. So tails is a live operating system also built to hide it to maintain your privacy and anonymity. Well then you can download and use tale's again this is a life operating the system which means you can boot it straight off a USB or a DVD and just run it from there. So it's been configured theoretically properly. And then there's also something called the Tor browser. So if you want to start to play around you know navigating the darknet. But you don't want actually to install Tor and go through all of that. You can download the Tor Browser Bundle. This is you download this, and you double click on the executable, and the TOR browser will run once the Tor Browser is running. Then within the Tor browser, the Tor browser itself connects to the TOR network, and then you can navigate the CNN dot com or whatever and keep your anonymity that way. Also if you want to play around it look in the dark the darknet or the deep web, and you don't want to install Tor. You can use this tor browser to be able to navigate. Now I've downloaded, and I've set up the Tor browser. So, if we go over. Here we can see that I have the Tor Browser already open so this isn't this isn't a full-fledged Tor. This is just the Tor Browser, and up here I want to show you. This is what one of those hidden services or darknet sites. What the quote-unquote what you call the domain name looks like it is just as horribly obnoxious whatever that is ".onion." So like I say a surfer surfing around the darknet. It's not like we sell illegal weapons dot onion. It's whatever this garbage is but this is what would be called a Website on the darknet a display Tor hidden service. And from here you can go on YouTube gambling and business and all the other kinds of stuff.

Now one of the things that I will tell you is I've been playing around with TOR all doing all this stuff and I find it to be noxious to use for the reasons I explained in the introduction to proxy classes. Proxies were hacked. Remember when you're hopping through that mesh of proxies you get slowed down by everybody else Internet connection so you may have 35 megabits per second up and down but the first relay may only have one megabit per second up and down, and the next relay might only have 756 56 Up and down and then the next relay may not may have a different speed. And so basically your speed is going to be whatever the slowest link is and then make it quite a bit slower than that. So when you're trying to use Tor to navigate around on the Internet again if you if you're trying to preserve your privacy if there is a reason that you're trying to do secretive stuff Hey spaghetti monster bless. Go for it. For me the average Joe. The NSA can figure out where I'm going.

They like to bounce through this network. Just I have found to be a bit agonizingly slow. But there you go. We are going to have a class on using these different products in installing and setting up Tor and Tor relays. However, just for this introduction class I just wanted to give you an overview so that you understood what is going on in Port relatively simplistic terms.

Again, in the modern era whether or not you should trust Tor. I'm not going to say I know a lot of people do trust Tor. So that's all fine for them. One of the things that I will warn you about with these hidden services these dark net Web sites is remembered the laws of your country are still valid even when you are on the darknet. One of the problems that I see with the darknet Web sites is people set up things like child porn people. People set up shop selling drugs. People set up a lot of bad stuff on the quote-unquote darknet. And remember if you go to the wrong site your web browser caches. Those pictures that you see on the wrong side and the police come knocking on the door.

Remember you will then, in fact, be in possession of CP possibly and you are going to suffer the jail time for that. So that is one of the things that it will warn you about the darknet Websites the secret services that the law does not stop once you start using Tor. Somebody figures out what you're doing. Can out all bunches of problems. So be careful there. Not only that but also people set up some nasty stuff on the darknet. So it is it is not necessarily something you want to be navigating through.

Q. Would you prefer Tails over Tor?

A. Basically what tails are tailed is a live operating system so you can boot this thing off of a DVD or a USB stick and it routes all of your data through the Tor network. Basically it's the equivalent of a Linux live CD It's built to just completely use the tour network. You don't have to worry about things like DNS supposedly you don't have to worry about things like DNS leakage or any of that kind of stuff. The question is then you guys know I am not a tor fan by any stretch of the imagination. One I just find it a pain in the butt to use Tor and to I just don't believe it.

It's like there is no privacy on the Internet.

There is no anonymity on the Internet.

The Internet functionally doesn't work that way. So I would argue that anybody that says that you can be anonymous online is blowing smoke up your ass. I mean it just functionally it's just functionally not built.

They'll compromise one of those servers so that when you go to that server even though you're using the Tor network, you can still download malware that will infect your computer with some spyware. Well this is NSA grade or KGB grade or whatever spyware. And the idea is so you go and you're doing whatever you're doing on the Tor network and then it's logging that information locally. And then what happens is when you drop off the tour network it will then beacon out to those agencies and say exactly who you are and where you've been. So on and so forth. So this is one of those things a lot of people don't think about you know when we're dealing with security. Security isn't over. It's a broad topic. There are a lot of things to deal with. Not only is it about encryption. Not only is it about hiding your IP address but it's also things like preventing software from being installed in your computer.

There is also something called a DNS leaking I talked about before. There are all of these other issues, and so one of the things is again is fundamentally compromising your computer through malware and then fund and sue.

So the idea then is you come up with a live CD seconds tales they get the benefit about using something like a live CD such as tails is that they can configure it pre-configured to make sure that there is no leakage. Right. So a DNS leakage basically this is a very interesting thing with the Tor network. That can happen is all of your Internet traffic gets routed over the Tor network but there is DNS leakage and what happens with DNS leakage is when you do a DNS query it goes out locally.

So you're at your computer you go to BBC dot com or P dot com. What happens is your computer accesses your normal ISP DNS gets the information and then when you go to the Web site that goes over the tor networks you get what's called DNS leakage. So if anybody is reading that DNS traffic they can see all the Web sites you're going to every to every time a Website has to be resolved to an IP address they can see what it's resolving to and that can be incriminating. So primarily by using something like tails alive, you can try to prevent that by massively configuring the live city not to allow that kind of stuff to happen.

The issue is though no.

You know the only time I would use tales. I mean in complete honesty is if I was going over to like use a friend's computer or I went into the office and I used the person besides me's computer to do something because.

Even when you're using tables even when you're using that life. And even when theoretically you can't get any malware or viruses on there. I don't believe that the data and all that can't be tracked. There's this whole thing with the NSA and these other intelligence agencies being able to compromise things like the exit nodes and the entrance nodes.

Moreover, there is an exciting idea where if these intelligence agencies can compromise enough nodes on the tour network that they can compromise both your entrance node and your exit node. That means they can read on your exit node they can mostly do a man in the middle attack to see all the data that's getting pulled into that exit node. Then if they're reading all the data that goes into the exit node and they control enough nodes, they can then match, and they can see the data flow from what's going in the exit node to what's coming out the entrance node. And so they can then match. And they can say OK we know that this exit node in this entrance node correspond we know the IP address that's connected to this entrance node is here. So we can then match that IP address to this entrance node to this exit node. And now we see all the data going back and forth. Right.

Again you're not getting compromised by malware, but you are getting compromised. Again the Tor network doesn't give a damn it really like I know it's cute. I know you want it to but, the only way I would use something like tails is if I was apprehensive about it may be like I was if I was travelling around the world and I was doing something a little weird and I went into like an Internet cafe.

I may be booed off of tables to do what I'm doing to give me a little bit added protection so that a local computer wasn't spying on me and the local data communication wasn't spying on me.

However, as far as like nation-state players in trying to keep your be anonymous from any of the big guys better tail Tales is better than having to install on your computer directly. It's better but not good. Better but not good is what I would say.

It just doesn't make sense. I wish I could bang that into people's heads. Functionally if you sit down with it, Tor doesn't.

A Conversation with KelvinSecTeam

Q. How would you define the dark web?

    A. There are pages and pages of flame wars going on the Internet, chat boards and boards are talking about go. This is the dark web; this is deep that there are many terms thrown around a dark web darknet deep web deep net and they're often used interchangeably, and they don't always mean the same thing. So formally if we're going to get kind of fussy about it, a darknet is a private overlay network where the connections are made only between trusted peers, and it's usually using non-standard protocols and ports. So darknet is a distinct from peer to peer networks because on darknets the tacit understanding that the presumption is that the sharing is going to be anonymous and so it's also sometimes called the deep net or deep web. Back in around 2,000 a computer scientist named Michael Bergman compared searching on the Internet to "dragging a net across the surface of the ocean"... A great deal might be caught in the net, but there's a wealth of information that's deeper and therefore missed by most of the search engine crawlers most of the Web's content is buried deep on site. Moreover, it's not indexed by standard search engines. So, those search engines don't find it. The portion that is indexed is called the surface web, and the dark web or the deep web that lies beneath it is several orders of magnitude larger than that.

Q. So how do you differentiate?

A. You know, for example, 30 years ago hacking or a hack was a good thing and now it's almost universally thought of as a bad thing at least by the general public. You know those negative connotation that it didn't have 30 years ago. Likewise a dark web dark net those didn't use to be necessarily associated with criminal intent but now that the common understanding when you when you talk about the dark web or the dark. That's it is understood that you are talking about that subset of non-index content that is also purposely anonymous and presumably hidden or possibly illegal.

Q. How does that tie into to feed intelligence?

A. Obviously to gathering intelligence is about you know getting information about what's out there and what's happening. Moreover, if you can't observe behavior by definition, you can't measure it or predict similar actions in the future. So when things are dark, it makes it hard to find them. Darknets have been the primary challenge for this new field of Internet security which is "threat intelligence," and it's definitely in protection probably you know the flavor of the month or the flavor of the year. However, there is still much confusion about what the borders of this base are and what those solutions do. The primary problem that is being worked in the intelligence business is it's easy to gather intelligence on the easily accessible indexed Internet; Google does it every day. What's harder and the stuff that's more interesting is the dark nets because that's where criminal intent and attacks are much more likely to emanate from. So we need to find ways to get in there with our flashlight and penetrate those very difficult to penetrate geographies and light up those darknet so that we can see what's happening in there because we're much more likely to find things that our customers will find interesting and helpful in terms of preventing future network attacks.

Q. How do you go ahead and do that?

A. You've hit on the core of why this has become a market. It's become a market because in the past there was no way to automate or take any shortcuts. Regarding indexing the darknet, you needed you to know individual computer scientists and network specialists that went out there by hand and hand penetrated and hand indexed own sites and dug and dug and hacked and hacked and hacked and then came back with a report. Many companies do this type of "Internet private investigative" work, "Internet PI," and they do it as a professional service and as a contract and that's great. However, companies that do professional services no matter how large they get rarely attract funding and almost never go public right.

A very successful company in the security space has to figure out how to automate something that used to be impossible to automate. So that's what the intelligence market is trying to do. We're trying to take these tasks that used to be impossible to do unless you hired precisely the right people to do them by hand either full time or by contract and create appliances portals and pieces of software that automate all or part of that search. So it uses a combination of new technologies new types of search engines and query languages that are specifically designed to dig down into that deep web and to discover content that wasn't discoverable before to find address spaces that aren't supposed to be exited.

You know that mainly IP spaces that are being squatted on but actually don't have any listings in the Internet directories automating things like penetrating vulnerabilities of Web sites are a perfect way of digging out content that is that its users or its population do not necessarily want to share with the rest of the world. Also, also the new types of applications like Tor and Tor to Web that help individuals and help bunnies find hidden files on the Internet in an automated way. Also, so the offerings that the IT security industry is putting together is trying to take that very labor intensive very specialized and esoteric knowledge which is how do I find out what's going on in this specific part of the darknets and automate that. I can say "hey you know what kinds of traffic are coming from the Dark Net?" in Bangladesh and my tool can help me catalogue all of the places that I should be looking at and you can at least you know shortening that cycle for me.

The supreme irony of the darknet is that it was set up by ARPA and in the military so that they could conduct a more secure and classify conversations and transactions over the public Internet. So you know basically, that's one of the reasons why it's so difficult to penetrate is that the technology doesn't have any backdoor is built into where it was it was designed to be secure and anonymous from the get-go. So the systems and the protocols that we're talking about are stable.

Q. Can it be used for good?

A. Absolutely. The darknets were indeed architected initially to be used for good instead of evil. You know specifically by governments and state security apparatus to combat terrorism and to keep information out of the hands of an enemy of a particular state you know, in more recent years darknets have been used as a platform for political dissidents and free speech activists the world over. So dissidents in countries with repressive regimes like North Korea have found that they can use some of the tools and apps and applications typical to the darknet to get their message out even on networks that are very tightly controlled by the state.

Q. Do you think that the government designed something that's too good even for them to infiltrate?

A. I think you know when these anonymity protocols were designed in the early 1970s the idea of everybody on the planet carrying around a computer in their pocket was it even the idea of a personal computer. It was, you know famously shot down by people over and over and over again they couldn't imagine why you would want in this room-filling machine in your house.

Mainly that these architects are at fault, they've designed something beautiful and substantial and provably anonymous, and they didn't create it with backdoors because it was intended for government and military use. It was explicitly designed to be secure. I don't think they ever imagined that three-quarters of the planet would have access to computers. Many orders of magnitude more potent than that the Apollo systems in their pocket. Good question for people that are shopping for threat intelligence services is starting to think about it. Threat Intelligence providers. I like to compare them to astronomers. Everyone's got in a slightly different telescope he or she's pointing to various pieces of the sky and some vendors some astronomers have lots of excellent infrared telescopes.

Other folks have great X-ray frequency telescopes, and other people do well in the visible light. So what you're seeing right now as the threat intelligence space kind of populates and matures is that different vendors are emerging with different specialities.

You know, and as far as intelligence concerned is concerned, one of the real hobbies is in deep penetration of the darkness. While that's certainly it is not the only intelligence we should be focused on, that's what is often advertised as a differentiator. Other intelligence companies will have different specialities, for example, might be good at digging up brand new malware samples. Malware is polymorphic this state these days, and the end replicates and mutates minute by minute, and just gathering all of those samples analyzing them figuring out what taxonomy they belong to and what their genetic heritage is and how much of a threat they are. That's a whole speciality in and of itself, and many companies focus more on say malware sample collection and other types of things that you can ask for from your threat intelligence companies are: what kinds of attacks do are you registering?

What kinds of traffic are you tracking?

Is this an intelligence company that is gathering intelligence from its customer networks for example at Symantec they'll claim to have an extensive threat intelligence network of hundreds of millions notes. What those nodes are customer machines and a guy who is running a bitcoin-based drug dealing site in South East Asia is not going to install a Symantec client on his computer because he knows he's going to show up on their intelligence network. Is your intelligence provider providing organic intelligence?

Building sensors of their own in hardware and or software and planting them out there on the Internet not on a customer's machine, building their private intelligence network and gathering that intelligence organically. Another thing to look for is what types of sensors these intelligence providers are making?

What about developing simulators that pretend to be something that they're not. They say, "I'm a card swipe machine that's really poorly configured," or "I'm an industrial controller," "I'm an intravenous machine at a hospital," I'm a PC, I'm a Mac, I'm a uranium centrifuge, and so on, simulate over a thousand different types of devices. So by looking at the intelligence network be able to tell what kinds of tools are being targeted. If there are specific types of devices are being targeted where those attacks are coming from and how it's trending. Also, so it's much easier for those vendors to batten down the hatches when it looks like there's a big Internet storm coming.

Q. What do you consider to be the most impactful lines of intelligence an organization can start to try to engage with it to deliver some immediate value and grow their security?

A. Part of part of the difficulty in building a real best practices intelligence organization in an IT company. The vertical industry. That's probably the farthest out front in this, are the banks and financial institutions, they are really at the forefront of utilizing intelligence sources.

A bank like says Barclays or Wells Fargo we'll tap into half a dozen or a dozen different intelligence sources to assemble a more holistic picture of the threats that are in front of them. However, some of this boils down to organizational best practice. I mean how are you as an organization and capturing the things that you already know about your network and the systems outside and how are you applying that knowledge. How well is the organization functioning organizations that are healthy and have good information flow and good information sharing between departments are much better set up to utilize a new source of intelligence that is not going to flood them with gigabytes of new data every minute you know. It's crucial that it the organization is prepared for that. Otherwise, it's just going to be you know piling more logs on top of more logs on top of more logs.

I think the thing that has surprised everyone in the security business is that sometime over the past 10 years while no one was looking all of the sudden security became a big data problem, and that caught many security professionals off guard because we've become excellent navel-gazers. We've been grown good at like looking inside of our networks and inside of our processes.

That's what's inside of my organization that's wrong that they need to fix to make it more secure. In the past 12–24 months you know the paradigms really flipped and now a lot of the forward-thinking security organizations are saying wow you know what we need to be doing is doing a lot more looking out the window, literally launching satellites seeing if there are hurricanes on the way. That kind of data will serve us much better in getting in our ROI out of our security budget. Because with that I can say this is a very stormy day on the Internet. Many attacks are targeting banks coming from Asia. You know what I'm going to screw the restrictions down tight on all of my security controls but just for the next few hours and then I'm going to ease them back again.

Q. So you tighten your security and you get a little bit more strict for just a few hours when you're under a specific and large amounts of attacks, and ease back when things clear up again that allows people to get they find they get a dramatically better catch rate and return on investment under existing security infrastructure.

A. Remember intelligence in and of itself doesn't make you secure. The value in buying threat intelligence is in making the security systems that you already have start paying for themselves. So the idea is that your firewalls, your intrusion prevention services, and so on, all of those get smarter work better and bug you less.

The intelligence service should take these vast piles of data and help your system's filter down the events so that they're only giving you facts that are genuinely crucial and truly important.

Q. What is a critical path to operationalise intelligence programs?

A. Organizations that have been successful at implementing threat intelligence have few common denominators we see organizations that are not afraid to experiment and fail fast. These are these are companies that are leaders and thought leaders and are willing to experiment with new technologies and do the types of experiments that can result in transformative moments from a from a security and intelligence perspective. We see organizations that are willing to invest in security.

They are the ones that are successful at threat intelligence. So, organizations and verticals that are hesitant to invest in security technology or they see security technology as a cost centre instead of at a profit centre are going to have a hard time. Also, companies that handle their knowledge and curate that and disseminate that in a well thought out organized and open fashion often do much better at implementing intelligence and getting good ROI out of the new threat intelligence technologies.

They can get great ROI because they know how to move information about situations around their organization and share that information across teams and that type of philosophy and approach is crucial to use threat Intelligence well. When you join the threat intelligence community you're going to find that there are lots of other people out there that are using threatened intelligence and that are getting attack data that is relevant and important to you, so you'll find large networks of companies that are set up correctly to share threat intelligence.

This is happening in the banking industry through organizations like FSI SAC and at the Department of Energy among American North American utilities in a program called Crisp.

Q. Is there any information that might be useful to get out the dark web?

A. Right now there aren't many offerings for say small and medium businesses in threat intelligence. This is still a big usually pretty expensive technology. So small and medium businesses don't have a good threat intelligence offering available to them yet at a price point that they can afford.

However, there is a lot of meta information that it that emerges from the threat intelligence fear that becomes published on things like the common vulnerability indexes or the various industry groups that collect and disseminate vulnerabilities and attack information. So even if you can't afford to buy a threat intelligence system for you for your medium-sized business, you can benefit from the development of threat intelligence technology, including publicly available reports on dark web scans and trends. Because what the technology and what the players in the field are doing, big banks that are using this technology they are surfacing attacks much more quickly much more reliably and on and on and much more standardized way so that the industry ... In general, is getting much better at delivering information to everybody in a predictable way that can be readily published on websites or read about. If you are a small-medium business and or you're just not ready to dive in to the threat intelligence pool, there are a lot of useful information sources on the Internet that can provide you with especially important alerts that your business should pay attention to keep an eye on the next common vulnerabilities and exploits list ... The CDC lists you can Google that, and also many industries have an Information Security Consortium that will publish relevant alerts and storm warnings for new types of zero days, hacks and large amounts of attack traffic coming from specific sources.

That information is all garnered from those members that do have threat intelligence system set up so as long as you're kind of you to know set up to receive those Amber Alerts or those flood warnings, you'll get them if you keep your eye on the correct Web sites. The insurance industry is a fascinating case study for what we're trying to do in threat intelligence because of the idea of insurance over the ensuing centuries.

Insurance companies have gotten very good at predicting a significant statistical basis over lots and lots of cargo ship trips which ships are going to go down or if not necessarily which ships are going to go down at least on average how many ships are going to go down in a specific fleet. So, again, we're kind of in metaphor land here. So far the security industry hasn't been very good at this. We haven't been very good at developing rigorous statistical and mathematical models for predicting networked incursions network failures or even the rates of those incursions or failures. So, the entrance of insurance companies into the cybersecurity market is a watershed moment.

A turning point for security as a discipline because frankly what's going to happen ... When the large businesses have even bigger budgets on the line, they are going to force a degree of rigor and mathematical sophistication that we haven't seen so far in the security industry, and they're going to want to know that they have made a good bet. Also, you're going to have to be able to prove it to them that they should write that policy for your company. One of the real critical areas of technological development in threat intelligence is, therefore, risk scoring.

How do we use 200 years of actuarial mathematical science that we developed in the insurance industry?

How do we apply those principles to a network and predicting what are the odds that this network is going to suffer added tactic and how do we adapt those algorithms so that we can look at a specific IP address for a particular URL and say "What are the odds that this IP address is dangerous?"

Alternatively, how risky would a connection with this IP address be if you know if I've never connected to it before, and I've got all of these data points saying that IP is located in Iran?

It wants to sell me products for free or SEO services. So all of these pieces fit into an actuarial algorithm consider something over 15 hundred different variables in that calculation, and we update that second by second for virtually every IP address on the Internet.

There is an enormous amount of computation that's going on a massive amount of re-crawling and re-scoring that a company would have to make to be sure that we can deliver real-time race-course that has a basis in actuarial science.

A Conversation with GmrB

Following is a conversation with black hat hacker GmrB (also known as Glorious MrBeast), which used to be popular on PasteBin and several other dark web forums for his tutorials on how to hide data and encrypt files.

The conversation happens over IRC chat after reaching out to GmrB on deep web social network Galaxy9.

Q. Tell me more about how you move information both online and offline? how you prefer to encrypt data?

A. I use Steghide, a command line tool to hide information in images. It only takes a few seconds to hide information in any file types. Some people call it "digital steganography." Steganography hides data in plain view, inside a file such as a photo or an audio track. As far as image files like JPEG or GIFs are concerned, to anyone unaware that it contains hidden data, it looks like just a normal picture. This method is particularly useful in countries where free speech is suppressed. Similar to digital watermarks used to find when images or audio files are not the originals.

Q. Tell me more about how you move information both online and offline? how you prefer to encrypt data?

A. The most common technique is called Least Significant Bit or LSB for short. The LSB process alters the last few bits in a byte to encode a message, which is especially useful in something like an image, where the red, green, and blue values of each pixel are represented by eight bits (one byte) ranging from 0 to 255 in decimal or 00000000 to 11111111 in binary. For example changing the last two bits in a completely red pixel from 11111111 to 11111101 only changes the red value from 255 to 253, which to the naked eye creates a nearly imperceptible change in color but still allows us to encode data inside of the picture. You can also design your own algorithm if you already have good coding and math foundations.

Q. What are the foundations of good digital stenography?

A. Encryption and Compression. Data encryption adds an extra layer of security, compression will allow you to fit more information in your "hidden file."

Q. Easier way to hide data in a file?

A. Use Steghide.

Q. Could you go into steps on how to install it? For example if a user is running Kali Linux, how would it work?

A. Ok, open the terminal and type:

apt-get install steghide
then type:

steghide embed -ef secretFile -cf coverFile -sf outputFile -z compressionLevel -e scheme

remember to use the correct arguments, here is a recent updated list for steghide arguments:

-ef specifies the path of the file that you want to hide. You can embed any kind of file inside of the cover file, including Python scripts or shell files.

-cf is the file that the data is embedded into. This is restricted to BMP, JPEG, WAV, and AU files.

-sf is an optional argument that specifies the output file. If this is omitted, the original cover file will be overwritten by your new steganographic file.

-z specifies the compression level, between 1 and 9. If you prefer not to compress your file, use the argument -Z instead.

-e specifies the type of encryption. Steghide supports a multitude of encryption schemes, and if this argument is omitted by default, Steghide will use 128-bit AES encryption, and you can also opt for no encryption.

Q. An example?

A. Type this:

steghide embed -ef SECRETMESSAGE.txt -cf YOURIMAGE.jpg -e none -Z

The example does not use any encryption or compression, it is just a test to show how steghide works. Once Steghide command is executed you will be prompted to set a password. Enter the password that will allow you to extract the embedded data later.

To retrieve the SECRETMESSAGE.txt hidden in the image use the command as follows:

steghide extract -sf stegoFile -xf outputFile

Once you run this command, you'll be prompted to enter the same password you created before. Then the extracted file will be the output. Sometimes you can find images with hidden messages via https://images.google.com/ which is not good if you are trying to keep your data securely hidden ….

Q. Talking about stenography: the TV series Mr. Robot shows the main character using a similar technique but using CDs. We can see him copying music to CDs, then embedding encrypted information on them that only he can recover. If anybody finds the CDs they will only be able to hear audio. Could you tell us a bit about that type of technique?

A. There are many types of softwares that can do that job easily, to name a few: AudioStegano, BitCrypt, MP3Stego ... I think a good alternative for a complete newbie would be DeepSound, it was developed for Windows.

Q. What would be the steps to use DeepSound?

A. Go to http://jpinsoft.net/DeepSound/Download.aspx and download the software. Deep Sound Interface is very straight forward. On the left you will see the directory structure of your C: drive and other drivers like USB devices. On the left you will see a list of files to use to hide your data. Click on the Settings icon in the top bar and select output director and output format. There are no mp3 file options right now, you will have to use.wav or .flac file formats, simply because .mp3 is a compressed format, we want to use a format that does not omit data.

DeepSound will use 256-bit AES encryption which is most common safe algorithm around.

Select the audio file you want to use, then open the data file you want to hide (I presume it is a .doc or .txt file) and select "Encode" icon on the top icon bar. Now you can go ahead and burn your CD, it will sound and look like a normal audio CD.

Q. How would you go about decrypt the content?

A. DeepSound will use the password you choose during encryption process (the longer the better) to secure your data. The person that has your password (or yourself) can decrypt the message/file encode in the audio file by selecting "Extract secret files" in DeepSound.

Q. I know you are involved in educating and training groups of hackers, what is your take on reconnaissance tools?

A. Sure, I would probably start with Nmap.

Q. In the case of a newbie with no experience with Nmap, what exercise or practice would you use to introduce intrusive Nmap scripts?

A. First, I have to mention that running Nmap scripts consumes a lot of CPU and bandwidth on the target web server, it may cause it to crash, break including launch denial of service attacks.

Second, we need to run the following command and I assume you are running Kali on a virtual machine or similar:

apt-get update && apt-get install nmap

Then run:

nmap --version

Nmap version (here will display version number, followed by platform type, and so on)

If you are lost, you can add --help to list all available options, for example one result when running nmap --help could be:
Nmap (version number) (https://nmap.org)

Usage: nmap [Scan Type(s)] [Options] {target specification}
TARGET SPECIFICATION:
Can pass hostnames, IP addresses, networks, etc.
Ex: scanme.nmap.org, microsoft.com/24, 192.168.0.1; 10.0.0-255.
1-254
-iL<inputfilename>: Input from list of hosts/networks
-iR <num hosts>: Choose random targets
--exclude <host1[,host2][,host3],...>: Exclude hosts/networks
--excludefile <exclude_file>: Exclude list from file
HOST DISCOVERY:
-sL: List Scan—simply list targets to scan
-sn: Ping Scan—disable port scan

-Pn: Treat all hosts as online -- skip host discovery

-PS/PA/PU/PY[portlist]: TCP SYN/ACK, UDP or SCTP discovery to given ports

-PE/PP/PM: ICMP echo, timestamp, and netmask request discovery probes

-PO[protocol list]: IP Protocol Ping

-n/-R: Never do DNS resolution/Always resolve [default: sometimes]

--dns-servers <serv1[,serv2],...>: Specify custom DNS servers

--system-dns: Use OS's DNS resolver

--traceroute: Trace hop path to each host

SCAN TECHNIQUES:

-sS/sT/sA/sW/sM: TCP   SYN/Connect()/ACK/Window/Maimon scans

-sU: UDP Scan

-sN/sF/sX: TCP Null, FIN, and Xmas scans

--scanflags <flags>: Customize TCP scan flags

-sI <zombie host[:probeport]>: Idle scan

-sY/sZ: SCTP INIT/COOKIE-ECHO scans

-sO: IP protocol scan

-b <FTP relay host>: FTP bounce scan

PORT SPECIFICATION AND SCAN ORDER:

-p <port ranges>: Only scan specified ports

    Ex: -p22; -p1-65535; -p U:53,111,137,T:21-25,80,139,8080,S:9

--exclude-ports <port ranges>: Exclude the specified ports from scanning

-F: Fast mode—Scan fewer ports than the default scan

-r: Scan ports consecutively—don't randomize

--top-ports <number>: Scan <number> most common ports

--port-ratio <ratio>: Scan ports more common than <ratio>

SERVICE/VERSION DETECTION:

-sV: Probe open ports to determine service/version info

--version-intensity <level>: Set from 0 (light) to 9 (try all probes)

--version-light: Limit to most likely probes (intensity 2)

--version-all: Try every single probe (intensity 9)

--version-trace: Show detailed version scan activity (for debugging)

SCRIPT SCAN:

-sC: equivalent to --script=default

--script=<Lua scripts>:<Lua scripts> is a comma separated list of
        directories, script-files or script-categories

--script-args=<n1=v1,[n2=v2,...]>: provide arguments to scripts

--script-args-file=filename: provide NSE script args in a file

--script-trace: Show all data sent and received

--script-updatedb: Update the script database.

--script-help=<Lua scripts>: Show help about scripts.
        <Lua scripts> is a comma-separated list of script-files or
        script-categories.

OS DETECTION:

-O: Enable OS detection

--osscan-limit: Limit OS detection to promising targets

--osscan-guess: Guess OS more aggressively

TIMING AND PERFORMANCE:

Options which take <time> are in seconds, or append 'ms' (milliseconds),

's' (seconds), 'm' (minutes), or 'h' (hours) to the value (e.g. 30m).

-T<0-5>: Set timing template (higher is faster)

--min-hostgroup/max-hostgroup <size>: Parallel host scan group sizes

--min-parallelism/max-parallelism <numprobes>: Probe parallelization

--min-rtt-timeout/max-rtt-timeout/initial-rtt-timeout <time>: Specifies
        probe round trip time.

--max-retries <tries>: Caps number of port scan probe retransmissions.

--host-timeout <time>: Give up on target after this long

--scan-delay/--max-scan-delay <time>: Adjust delay between probes

--min-rate <number>: Send packets no slower than <number> per second

--max-rate <number>: Send packets no faster than <number> per second

FIREWALL/IDS EVASION AND SPOOFING:

-f; --mtu <val>: fragment packets (optionally w/given MTU)

-D <decoy1,decoy2[,ME],...>: Cloak a scan with decoys

-S <IP_Address>: Spoof source address

-e <iface>: Use specified interface

-g/--source-port <portnum>: Use given port number

--proxies <url1,[url2],...>: Relay connections through HTTP/SOCKS4 proxies

--data <hex string>: Append a custom payload to sent packets

--data-string <string>: Append a custom ASCII string to sent packets

--data-length <num>: Append random data to sent packets

--ip-options <options>: Send packets with specified ip options

--ttl <val>: Set IP time-to-live field

--spoof-mac <mac address/prefix/vendor name>: Spoof your MAC address

--badsum: Send packets with a bogus TCP/UDP/SCTP checksum

OUTPUT:

-oN/-oX/-oS/-oG <file>: Output scan in normal, XML, s|<rIpt kIddi3, and Grepable format, respectively, to the given filename.

-oA <basename>: Output in the three major formats at once

-v: Increase verbosity level (use -vv or more for greater effect)

-d: Increase debugging level (use -dd or more for greater effect)

--reason: Display the reason a port is in a particular state

--open: Only show open (or possibly open) ports

--packet-trace: Show all packets sent and received

--iflist: Print host interfaces and routes (for debugging)

--append-output: Append to rather than clobber specified output files

--resume <filename>: Resume an aborted scan

--stylesheet <path/URL>: XSL stylesheet to transform XML output to HTML

--webxml: Reference stylesheet from Nmap.Org for more portable XML

--no-stylesheet: Prevent associating of XSL stylesheet w/XML output

MISC:

-6: Enable IPv6 scanning

-A: Enable OS detection, version detection, script scanning, and traceroute

--datadir <dirname>: Specify custom Nmap data file location

--send-eth/--send-ip: Send using raw ethernet frames or IP packets

--privileged: Assume that the user is fully privileged
--unprivileged: Assume the user lacks raw socket privileges
-V: Print version number
-h: Print this help summary page.
EXAMPLES:
nmap -v -A scanme.nmap.org
nmap -v -sn 192.168.0.0/16 10.0.0.0/8

Etc.

Q. We have mentioned hiding data in files, can we use nMap to extract
   data from files?

A. Yes. http-exif-spider script can be used to extract data from photos
   found on websites. It looks for EXIF data in graphic files: personal
   blogs, small businesses, and corporate organizations often forget
   to "clean" graphic files before they are posted. EXIF is short for
   EXchangeable Image File: either device information, GPS coordi-
   nates, timestamps, and so on, that gets stored in JPEG, PNG and
   even PDFs.

   A lot of photos on Internet contain GPS data. Instagram,
   Twitter, and Facebook because they scrub EXIF data every time
   users upload new photos. Check the "Higinio Ochoa arrest" to see
   a classic example of what type of issues unsafe upload of photos to
   Internet can cause.

   Higinio Ochoa arrest:

   For example if I use ports 80 and 443 (-p80,443), very common
   web server ports, as my ports for a EXIF Spider attack, I would run:

   nmap -p80,443 --script http-exif-spider NameOfTheWebsiteYou-
   WantToTarger.com

   The result should look something like this:

Starting Nmap 7.70 (https://nmap.org)

Nmap scan report for targetWebsite.com

Host is up (0.11s latency).

PORT   STATE SERVICE

80/tcp open http

| http-exif-spider:

| http://NameOfTheWebsiteYouWantToTarger.com:80/Image.jpg

| Make: SAM CORPORATION

| Model: SAM E1

| Date: 2018:05:12 13:00:02

| http://NameOfTheWebsiteYouWantToTarger.com:80/image2.

jpg

| Make: APP CORPORATION

| Model: APP I1

|_   Date: 2018:05:12 13:00:12

443/tcp open https

| http-exif-spider:

| https://NameOfTheWebsiteYouWantToTarger.com:443/image3.

jpg

| Make: C CAMERA

|_   Model: CAMERA MODEL 1

Nmap done: 1 IP address (1 host up) scanned in 40.03 seconds

If you receive error message "Current http cache size exceeds max size." You will have to increase the nMap cache size. Large image files are hard to work, use http.max-cache-size to increase the size, for example ("78999999" is a completely random number):

nmap -p80,443 --script http-exif-spider --script-args="http.max-cache-size=78999999" NameOfTheWebsiteYouWantToTarger.com

Q. Of course nMap can be used for a more features, for example bypass trigger web application firewalls or alert system administrators. Best online resource on nMap?

A. Check out https://nmap.org/nsedoc/scripts/http-exif-spider.html and alternatives/more advanced tools like Angry IP Scanner, Win-MTR, Fing and Zenmap on Linux.

Hiring a Hacker on Galaxy9

Q. You (GmrB) as a Black hat have just discovered you can upload WAR files to a web server what do you do (you are in their LAN)

A. Upload a shell and enter the server through that shell.

Q. What is one attribute from a Straight and a Crossover cable?

A. Straight, for example:

1. Connect a computer to a switch/hub's standard port.
2. Connect a computer to a cable/DSL modem's LAN port.
3. Connect a router's WAN port to a cable/DSL modem's LAN port.
4. Connect a router's LAN port to a switch/hub's uplink port (generally used for expanding network).
5. Connect 2 switches/hubs with one of the switch/hub using an uplink port and the other one using a standard port.

alternatively, Crossover:

1. Connect 2 computers directly.
2. Connect a router's LAN port to a switch/hub's standard port (generally used for expanding network).
3. Connect 2 switches/hubs by using a standard port in both switches/hubs.

Q. You are tasked with physically penetrating a door of an office building only one problem, there is a movement detector on the other side how do you get in? (there is a gap between the doors)

A. The doors can be opened by getting a canister of compressed air, by sliding the nose (whatever it's called) through the gab you can spray toward the detector, and the doors will open.

Q. What is a significant difference between TCP and UDP

A. UDP doesn't have error-checking, TCP does have error-checking

Q. For what reason would you boot from your network adapter instead of your drive with an OS on it? (Internetworking perfectly)

A. If you want an image of an OS you will do this to receive the image of the OS over the network. (does need WDS server or something similar)

Q. Give the HEX for, occupied space on a disk, free space (after a program was deleted), totally free (no previous program was here)

A. ff ff = occupied space on disk e5 = free space (after program was deleted) 00 00 = totally free (no previous program)

Q. Why would you not want to use symmetric encryption?

A. Because you are using the same key to encrypt and decrypt the message if this key were to be stolen all your messages would be decryptable.

Q. When do you deploy spear-phishing over regular phishing?

A. Spear-phishing is targeted toward a particular person, while phishing is not targeted against an individual

CICADA 3301

A conversation with Th Stg

11: AM, September 2018, Hunters Point, San Francisco, CA.

It is a bright cold morning, and I'm approaching the public phone booth at the end of Galvez Avenue, right after the Storehouse Coffee to get the call from Cicada 3301.

Hunters Point is one of two major neighborhoods in the southeastern corner of San Francisco. The name brings back memories of the Vice documentary on the Bayview area, the locals call it "San Francisco's radio-active basement."

I didn't know much about Cicada 3301 up until then I started a communication with some of the members after a series of private messages exchange over Twitter.

During early September 2018, a Twitter user called Lestat introduced me to Cicada 3301 members Th Stg and Revolutionary Fox.

I got interested in the Cicada 3301 group because of the puzzles and because of the symbology of their amazing YouTube videos, in particular, my fascination with the Cicada 3301 group is related to their message, they seem to be not interested in rebellion at all. It seems to connect to a "technological renaissance." An inspirational message for the new generations.

They want to try to wake up the current and next generations. Using the languages of arts, entertainment and technology and disclosing and a showing the real truth behind all the manufactured, and low-quality information that we constantly receive through the mass media channels.

The group is known to be a group that collects genius's from many different disciplines. They remain anonymous, and hold Privacy sacred.

Unlike other groups, they do not actively rebel against authority, and as a group dedicated to privacy, it is ironic how quickly their intriguing message is permeating cyberspace and attracting devotees.

I am waiting for the phone call, not knowing it will be the first of a series of arranged calls about Cicada 3301 and its mission. The funny thing is that I didn't have any proper equipment to record the phone call. So after about 10 minutes, I decided to give up on the recording and the leader of Cicada 3301 very kindly agrees to have another phone call on the following day. So during the first day, we have a private conversation of about two hours where we go through anything from alchemy to science from psychology to quantum physics and classical physics. And we go deep into discussions about the founder of Debian Linux and his controversial death, and also details on how human beings behave when they're exposed to the truth. During the second day, at an earlier time around 9am. I have the second phone call with the Cicada 3301 leader. And this time we focus our conversation on the Cicada 3301 group and we explore the values of the group. We don't really touch anything that is technology related but I have found the phone call to be extremely valuable because of the information that it provides about the Cicada 3301 group. In particular, because it provides a clear, direct and honest description of the group purposes and what the trying to achieve. The following transcription is this the Cicada 3301 approved transcription of the phone call recorded on the second instance of interaction.

Following is the transcription of a phone interview with Th Stg on the mission, philosophy and inspiration behind Cicada 3301.

Q. What is Cicada 3301?

A. We are a movement to some and a destiny to others. Our goal is to try to teach people self-reliance and preserve privacy.

Imagine that the world is an ocean, your mind and your soul are a raft, your body is mineral and vegetative. So your raft could be a micro environment, you can teach a raft how to steer, you can shelter on the surface of a raft, or you can build a fire on the surface of the raft and find warmth, and nourishment. You can boil the poisonous salt from the very waters that support your raft. What we are trying to do is to teach people how to program their own minds.

We are born into an environment where governments want us to think in a certain way, want them to procreate at a certain time, wants to dominate how we think politically, wants to know how we spend money and when and where they spend money. They want to control our lives.

Do you really think they will not stop until they can read and control every process of thought going through our raft?

Is it wise to fight them on their own battlefield, using weapons they created? Or do we choose a new path where we create our own worlds, our own thoughts, our own devices to tune out their constant propaganda?

Q. Ok, so it is a message to awake people, by understanding the value of freedom and also privacy?

A. Very, very good.

It is also what you just said, privacy is sacred.

Privacy is a right, and we are on the road to have privacy being criminalized as already happened in Turkey and China, elements of privacy are criminalized here in the first world too.

Q. Probably we have a difference between how privacy is criminalized in the third world compared to the first world. In the third world privacy is criminalized and in certain circumstances controlled using violence, while in the first world privacy is regulated and controlled using processes and regulations.

I have encountered in various definitions of privacy, one being the definition of privacy as per core member of the Tor project Jacob Appelbaum description, "the freedom to have an open, unmonitored." In Appelbaum definition privacy goes hand in hand with freedom. What is your definition of privacy?

A. I would mention science fiction writer Philip K. Dick, who died in 1982 also, which underlines in his work how the lack of privacy causes discomforts of all sorts for societies, also psychologically diseases. You need privacy not only for conversations, but also for creativity, procreation, to be able to have introspective time.

Nothing is private if everything is open, and what you have is persistent 24 hours seven day a week herd mentality. You don't have time to know your own personality, your own ideas.

Q. Sometimes we see privacy being portrayed in the wrong way in the Western world, as a something synonymous of "things to hide" or "bad things to hide" or "unnecessary need to hide." A completely opposite compete to "respect communication in freedom," and understanding that without free speech growth would not be possible.

A. Yes, absolutely. I agree.

Q. One thing that a lot of people noticed about the amazing visuals, music and content, in general, both on YouTube and Twitter by Cicada 3301 is the language you use. A language independent from other movements or groups of activists and "hactivists" such as Anonymous and Wikileaks. There is no feeling of rebellion in Cicada, it transpires that you are not trying to rebel, rather want to inspire people. Make people think instead of make them react.

A. Rebellion takes energies that are deleterious to our outlet. We want to be different from the other movements, we want people to focus on introspection. Focus on the internal psyche.
"Render unto Caesar the things which are Caesar's."
We seek our own internal enlightenment through introspection. And of course, you need privacy to have introspection. So, it is linked.
We are nothing like Wikileaks or Anonymous, that is not our focus. We respect both "organizations," we are "wonder and wandering." Imagination and pilgrimage.

Q. Cicada 3301 has mentioned about the work of Bruno Borges, who has released 14 encrypted books and several other books as inspiration. Would you have any work you would like to highlight?

A. That would be a long list. Let me start by saying that Bruno is with us, and what he composed was the Liber Secundus. I personally get inspired by the works of William Blake, in particular "The Marriage of Heaven and Hell," "Self-Reliance" by Ralph Waldo Emerson and my all time favorite, The Glass Bead Game.

What I have been starting to do recently is to dive deeply into forbidden books of the late middle ages, when the Church forced philosophy and alchemy underground. For example, books written during the period of Inquisitions.

I also enjoy Kurt Vonnegut, Orson Welles and also enjoy the works of Philip K. Dick.

Q. Other books I might have seen mentioned as sort of inspiration for Cicada 3301 are the Book of Enoch by John Dee and Simulacra and Simulation by Jean Baudrillard. Do you think the common pattern between those books is to find freedom by transcending reality? Do you think there is a common pattern?

A. I do.

You mentioned John Dee. Dee and Edward Kelley or Kelly, also known as Edward Talbot, who we don't know a lot about, who supposedly purchased several magic books and helped John Dee in rituals and esoteric practices. If we took Dee works, for example "Monas Hieroglyphica," those books are about "incantations." Incantations with a common goal, which is enlightenment.

I read a lot about awakening; we have lost touch with Mother Nature. We need to embrace the path to allow us bypass our blockages.

Q. You have mentioned about a "block." Some people have speculated we have blocks wired in our genetic code. The ancient Sumerian myth of Enûma Eliš, inscribed on cuneiform tablets, the legendary Anunnaki, the Sumerian deities, whom genetically altered the human race with a pre-programmed block to limit the "human hybrid" access ESP and SSP perception. A similar link is present in the "original sin" in the Bible and in many Eastern philosophies where enlightenment can only be achieved by breaking through an "invisible veil." Do you think the work of Cicada 3301 would allow people to bypass this block, or do you think there is no block at all?

A. I do think there is a block. I also think that the information to access a solution to bypass those blockages is freely available around us but we need to be open to "see it." There is a pilgrimage in seeking enlightenment. When you first find truth, it troubles and vexes you, until you realize the same truth lie dormant inside of you for longer than you realize.

Q. It comes to mind the work of two very different scientists: Richard Dawkins and Rupert Sheldrake. Dawkins fascination with the study on how cultural information spreads (who coined the name "meme" to describe a unit of information residing in the brain and that mutates and replicates in human cultural evolution) and Sheldrake concept of "morphogenetic fields" (the phenomenon where a group of cells able to respond to discrete, localized biochemical signals leading to the development of specific morphological structures or organs.) when studying the evidence that as more and more people learn or do something it becomes easier for others to learn or do. Both concepts mention about the universal law of feedback.

Do you think forms of communications and cultural growth either via "memes" or trough "resonance" are blocked or badly influenced by the human ego? I have noticed several mentions to "ego-death" in relation to Cicada 3301 online. What is your version in relation to "transcend the ego"? Should we transcend our own egos?

A. One hundred percent yes. Although transcend the ego is only possible temporally. Ego is a component of survival; however, ego is also what institutions use against you by both appealing to it and crushing it when they find it necessary.

Think of propaganda and prison. Both speak to ego no?

Q. What is the current stage of Cicada? Will we see more puzzles or will you focus on open education messages?

A. There will be more challenges.

Q. During July 2015 a group called themselves "3301" and claimed to have hacked Planet Parenthood, creating confusion between the real Cicada 3301 and false actors. The use of PGP encrypted messages also increased the confusion in relation to heavy secrecy around Cicada 3301. Could you tell me more in relation to the misinformation around Cicada 3301?

A. That was not the first time, we deny any relation to them.

Q. We live in a time where technology is evolving faster than us, technology is directly influencing us in the way we communicate, think and behave. When people think about technology they think about knowledge; considering the dichotomies between concepts like chaos and noise, knowledge and imagination … how would you envision a time where people associate technology with imagination?

A. If you take obesity in the first world, many people would blame food. They are not completely incorrect, food is one of the root causes, but also improper use of technology is in the list of causes.

Technology and its results are meant to help us and somehow "augment our senses," but if we do not know how to use technology we will have technology owning us. We have grown obese in part because we sit and expect technology to do our jobs for us, so the actual functionality of our bodies grows less important and you see weight gain as a result.

Q. It seems that in the Western world "technology owns people," while in places like Japan, people and technology are one thing (and sometimes vice versa). Do you think we will enter a "technological renaissance?"

A. I think that there will be new renaissances. The Bonfire of the Vanities (February 7, 1497) was a attack by controllers to crush an enlightenment movement. The world is made up of those who wish to control us, and those who wish to be free … the contributions of the de Medici family to the Renaissance in Italy spread a fire no repressive priest could stop … however, history repeats itself in cycles and this relates to periods of creative flowering.

I do think we will have many technological renaissances ahead, as we already have. The advent of gunpowder brought a massive plague upon Europe and Asia. It's always prosperity followed by complacency followed by war. Look at the new generations, they will undergo physical mutations in the coming centuries because of the influence of technology in our everyday life; it reminds me of speculative theories such as the aquatic ape theory of Toeffler where human have lost their hair trough swimming the oceans after having to climb down from the trees of a vanishing forest.

I do not agree with claims that humankind is fully evolved now, I think that humans will constantly keep evolving through time, and we are only at the beginning of our infancy of how we will think and look in a million of years.

Right now, there is a bit of a race between AI and humankind, we might have to figure out how to manage technology if and when it would get close to resemble or mimic biological organisms and potentially become a physical threat for us. As you pointed out, if we program a survival instinct into AI, AI will bite the hand that feeds it.

Q. How important is the music aspect in the Cicada 3301 language? The language of sound organized in time and space, a universal language.

A. We believe that music transcends reality and allows to access higher level of existence. Think about translating communication in chants, songs and musical mantras, repetitive patterns along with percussive elements, You see this in different cultures, we see it in Native Americans, Aborigines, and so on, cultures that approach sound through "musical shamanism." People love our music and the combination of music and visuals. These are powerful tools in the hands of individuals quest for pilgrimage for enlightenment.

Music speaks to our spirit.

Music can be heard inside your head, heart and soul. What other medium can permeate like this?

We are developing a new language that will be music centric. More on that when you write your next book my friend.

Q. What is the key to decipher the Da Vinci code?

A.

Atlayo

A Conversation with Mr. Security

This chapter is the result of a random e-mail I have received on my Tor2Box account after posting the following comment on the dark web social network Atlayo (at the time, accessible both on the deep and clear net):

> *Looking for white, grey, red or black hats to interview on topics of privacy, security and deep web for my upcoming book. DM me or e-mail me for details. PGP details below.*

The e-mail (sent from "MrSecurity@TheUnknowns.xyz") was signed by a user called "MrSecurity." Up until then, I was not sure about the link between "MrSecurity@TheUnknowns.xyz" and the ethical hacking group "The Unknowns," which came to attention in 2012 after a series of cyber attacks to NASA, CIA, White House, the European Space Agency, Harvard University, and several ministries of defence. The whole content of the e-mail is centred on the Podesta Case, and the techniques used during the infamous spear-phishing attack initially attribute to cyber espionage group Fancy Bear (also known as APT28, Pawn Storm, Sofacy Group, Sednit and STRONTIUM).

Hi,

My name is MrSecurity.

I am a researcher, security expert and privacy supporter.

I decided to reply to your message on Atlayo with my view on the Podesta case and which things unfolded during 2016.

First, you must understand that e-mail has become the lifeblood of communication on the Internet ever since folks realized they had a way to get in touch across time zones and set up ways to send information asynchronously. People over the age of 30 cannot comprehend trying to organize any jobs electronically. Its drawbacks, deficiency of encryption, the difficulty of verifying senders' identities, potential for being tapped at some stage on the way, and the problem of knowing if a receiver has received it or read it, have been solved with other systems, which offer encryption, affirmation and delivery/read receipts. Still, e-mail endures the Internet's cockroach.

However, if you're conducting a US presidential campaign, you'd require an e-mail—would not you?

A campaign is a tremendously complicated undertaking. There are teams across the US at the local level, and also the need to both tailor messages to different nations and neighborhoods, allied to have a message for newspapers and TV. Moreover, in the first phases, the struggle isn't against another party; it is against a rival from the same party so that messages and speeches need to be subtly tweaked to appeal to the existing voters, not the swing voters at the broader nation. Coordinating what is mentioned, and when, is crucial. Secrecy, too, matters: in announcing initiatives permitting the other side know what you're planning would let them prepare their response, or just beat you to the punch. Countless millions of dollars have been spent chasing the job in the world. It is not a company for amateurs. In January 2015, Hillary Clinton hired John Podesta, who'd just turned 66, as her campaign manager, and her chief of staff for the effort once she announced she had been running. They understood each other nicely: Podesta was President Bill Clinton's chief of staff from October 1998 to January 2001, managing a period of crises which comprised impeachment proceedings. Those started in December 1998 and declared a time in American politics. Afterwards, Podesta had worked for President Obama, also was a visiting professor of law at Georgetown University. In summary, he had been through it. In April 2015 Hillary Clinton declared (via YouTube) her next attempt to become the Democratic candidate for president.

After a winter effort, she was left by the outcome of the first Democratic primary in Iowa on 1 February 2016 unexpectedly in a race from 74-year-old Bernie Sanders, six years her senior touting a schedule that culminated with younger voters. Six weeks later, on 15 March, Clinton won the Democratic primaries in Missouri, Ohio, North Carolina, Florida and Illinois—but by narrow margins, notably just 0.2 percent of votes in Missouri. There would be primaries in Utah, Idaho and Arizona which would favor Sanders though Clinton had obtained candidates that are enough to wrap up the nomination.

The pressure was tremendous.

Clinton was at the direct on delegates—but the campaign was unsettled by Sanders' determination and the degree of support that he had been drawing. Though members of Clinton's team kept an eye on it the Republican Party's problems using the insurgent candidacy of Donald Trump seemed far away. In an effort team containing hundreds of individuals, such as a business, Clinton was comparable to the executive, also Podesta efficiently the chief operations officer, responsible for making everything run smoothly.

From the team, the organization fanned with one goal: getting Hillary Clinton elected president in November, a complex web of interlocking tasks, into topic-based and state-based groups.

Podesta was directing operations that included determining to downplay and which countries to visit, what policies to encourage, and collecting "opposition research" about likely opponents, both at the main stage and the head-to-head race for the tape.

There was also within the effort to some extent a generational split. Those at the top had grown up and seen the Internet grow from an academic oddity for this year's miracle and into a part both of them and coordinating. Those at the bottom were part of a smartphone production to which the net was a background hum.

They were used to programs like Facebook and Snapchat. However, organization and the effort's thinking flowed from the people brought in to help arrange it, and from the top. What everybody knew was that safety mattered. In an age of anti-virus and of Wikileaks—that had published thousands of leaked US government e-mails (or "wires") from 2010—you needed to guard your electronic data as closely as possible. Thus the e-mail that appeared Saturday, 19 in Podesta's inbox March 2016 was about.

The "From:" address was "no-reply@accounts.googlemail.com," a legitimate sender e-mail for Google. The subject line said: "*Someone has your ."

The content was just as worrying. "Someone gets your password" it stated in the text that is white, in a box with a backdrop.

"Hi John," the message continued below, in plain text.

It then detailed a clear attempt from Ukraine to get the account: the IP address matched that of a cell phone operator that was Ukrainian.

"Google stopped this effort. You need to change your password."

It then offered a link.

Right from the start, one of the most significant problems for Clinton's campaign staff had been the persistence of media coverage about "her e-mails."

During her 2008 presidential campaign bid, a private e-mail server had been set up in the family house in New York. In 2009 she had been forced secretary of state, nevertheless kept using the server for accessing e-mails. In 2013 the server was moved to a data centre in New Jersey.

In August 2015 when it became clear that Clinton was using the machine for a mixture of official and non-official business, the FBI began an investigation. Because the effort lasted, together with former security chiefs suggesting the host was hacked to spill secrets that were rumbling on in the spring of 2016.

It seemed apparent, although they didn't have any evidence. Clinton scoffed at the notion, suggesting that there were no signs of a breach, and nothing stored on it. However, the problem for the campaign was that the words Clinton' and "e-mails" at a newspaper headline would suck at focus away from anything else until the FBI investigation was resolved. Due to the general election, that looked increasingly sure to be as the Republican candidate, the campaign group against Donald Trump was on advantage over anything connecting the words "e-mail" and safety. Trump had imputed to it. It had been imputed to by sanders. When it came to safety, what you didn't want was somebody by rifling through your e-mails sabotaging it.

Along with the Clinton campaign didn't need any publicity about hacking and e-mails. It was 2.34 a.m. in San Francisco, in which he had been staying with a buddy, before flying back to Washington, DC's Reagan Airport in the day. On the east shore, people were already up and in the Clinton headquarters at Brooklyn.

As is typical for high-level members of an effort, three or more people had access to the personal inbox of Podesta, including his chief of staff.

Can it be something that Podesta needed to be worried about? Not sure.

When his e-mail had been compromised, there was. Alternatively, was it a phishing e-mail—by tricking him with an authentic-looking e-mail something trying to receive his login details?

Phishing has a long, glorious history.

In September 1995, America Online was the US's biggest Internet service provider: Steve Case, its chief executive, proudly declared that there were a remarkable 3.5 million members. However, Case had some news that is concerning: users would be asked to change their passwords regularly because hackers were trying—and success. "There were some instances where people are passing themselves off as workers or agents and asking members" "This was not AOL policy; he explained: under no circumstances will anyone from AOL ever request your password." The hackers, meanwhile, had industrialized the procedure of capturing these details from users who were new to the Internet and unschooled in the pitfalls of communication.

The hackers would send messages to novice users through AOL Instant Messenger or e-mail, posing as AOL staff and requiring individuals to confirm their details. Usually their username and password, and for good measure title, address, credit card number, bank name and expiry date, for vague reasons ("We've detected hackers using your accounts... We have lost your account info... We didn't receive your billing information...").

Though many of those would dismiss them would bite and hand it had been rewarding for the natives. The clinic was known as phishing— because everyone used dial-up connections on their telephone lines, fishing using a telephone spin—and also the earliest recorded use of the term appears to have been in February 1996. Phishing wasn't, and is not, hacking at the strict sense; there's no subversion of a computer. Instead, the subversion is of the consumer's anticipation of what the computer will show them.

We expect that because the computer is reliable, it won't let messaging that is false to appear; which in precisely the same way it disturbs Internet address or a malformed e-mail, it will identify a site or an e-mail. However, computers only do what they're told, and they dutifully will when they are advised to display a message intended to deceive the reader.

The problem was always to educate consumers in what was real and what was fake, and how to guarantee that individuals would not fall for the latter. It easy for any web developer that is competent to replicate the HTML for any login page, but with all the entrance fields linked to their collection points.

It looks real but isn't.

The increase in the use of SSL, which certifies the security of a link to a website, as well as browsers that could use the SSL certificate to determine if or not a site was masquerading, helped; but people didn't always understand what signs to look for.

Phishing did not go away.

By 2015, Canada's government estimated 156 million phishing e-mails were being sent daily, of 8 million could be opened and which 16 million could reach people's inboxes.

Of those, one in ten, or 800,000, would click the hyperlinks and their details would be entered by one in ten of those in the site that is phishing.

That is only a 0.05 percent success rate, but it is still 80,000 daily. Overall, they found 12.4 million credentials phished.5 Even so, that paled compared to the number of credentials exposed by data breaches, which equates to 1.9 billion. The issue that poses because of safety is that usernames can be guessed, or so are often public. (Often they are just an e-mail address.)

Passwords can be drawn out of a limited number of personalities, and people tend to want to choose something which they can remember. This makes encrypted passwords exposed to a "dictionary attack" where a computer slogs through possible combinations of characters and existing words, running them through the same algorithm that encrypted the password that is initial, to attempt to locate a match.

The debut of high-performance graphics processing units (GPUs) has become a blessing for password cracking since they can perform simple applications at exceptional speeds.

A phishing attack which somebody uses may give access to a lot of their other people. Phishing has been categorized into a variety of forms, such as whaling (aimed in the biggest, often wealthiest, goals), and "spearphishing," targeting particular individuals in business due to their position.

E-mails that pretend to be from someone within the business and also have links to malicious websites or "invoices" delivered to accounts sections whose fasteners are now malware are a frequent type of assault. When somebody else gets phished, the trend is to think they are fools; however, once you get phished, it is because you're caught off guard, or it is the service supplier's fault for not getting greater protections against imitation logins. It is always about trust. Successful malware is about hitting on the buttons that are right.

An e-mail was sent out by his staff with the subject line "SEAL group six conducts." Alternatively, did somebody have access to the e-mails of Podesta?

Within half an hour that he responded: "This is a valid e-mail. Make sure that authentication is switched on his accounts, and John should change his password immediately."

Two-factor authentication (2FA) has been an additional layer of safety for any account generally shielded only by a password and username.

When you attempt to log in from a new apparatus, it needs a code that's sent individually to, or created on, an already reliable apparatus.

The ring of reliable devices or programs is subsequently widened either by creating one-time passwords to be employed on particular devices or inputting the password followed with an authorization code' created utilizing a program or delivered by the server to your telephone and then usually is valid for approximately 30 minutes. Once set up, 2FA tends to remain out of this way; it does not interfere with accessing or sending e-mail, or registering to a social networking or other accounts, provided that you are doing this on a device is already given your imprimatur.

When you are attempting to log to an apparatus that is new or alternative, does this become a roadblock? (To guard against the chance that you have dropped your phone and do not have access to some other trusted apparatus, Google and many others allow you to create "anytime codes" to print out and maintain.)

However, the roadblock for you becomes an impenetrable wall to get a hacker. Should they require a one-time code that is transmitted to a device (itself usually guaranteed by a different, distinct code, or biometrics), hacking to the accounts becomes a much different challenge?

Find a code which will enable them, or the only way around it is to steal the apparatus. Finding the code is not simple. The code created by an app on your telephone, or delivered to the telephone of the owner and can be created by the login server. The code is created by a "seed" amount offered by the server, which is read to the program typing in a succession of characters or by scanning a QR code. When the user attempts to log into, the program and the server equally employ a predetermined algorithm working with the seed along with the moment, to the nearest 30 seconds, to create a 40-character code that is then boiled down to some six-digit number.

Enter that amount, and you are in.

Every 30 seconds, there'll be an amount; you cannot forecast what the number is without even understanding that the seed. In theory, provided that the seed remains protected within the program and on the host, the consumer has been authenticated by you. Well, nearly. The dilemma is that the host allows for your device's clock to float somewhat, and computes not only the present code but also the code to your prior 30-second section, also for the subsequent one.

This produces a window for hacking. It is relatively easy to construct a page that resembles Gmail login, and asks for a code and moves those components on into the actual Gmail page. Such a "man in the middle" attack lets the user confirm their system contrary to Gmail's challenge; today they are logged in and have caught the user's password (that has only been typed in) so that they could get the e-mail settings to catch a pair of anytime codes.

However hacking a 2FA-protected account isn't trivial, and should the malware is not done well it'll trigger suspicion both in the e-mail supplier as well as the consumer who's being phished. Generally, 2FA lowers the prospect of being murdered by 90 percent or more, and should you attempt to phish somebody without recognizing that they've 2FA switched on, the credentials that you receive are useless.

Nevertheless, roughly 70 percent of e-mail users do not utilize 2FA, as shown by a poll of 2,000 adults in May 2016. Just more than half weren't sure how it worked; 41 percent had no clue what it was. This means hackers can depend on seven recipients of the phishing e-mails with no security provided that they click through the bogus page and enter their login information. Podesta's private Gmail accounts were one of those 70 percents: it did not have 2FA allowed. Delavan afterwards said he had mistyped in his response to Latham: he had meant to mention it had been an illegitimate e-mail, maybe not a valid one. In his response to Latham, he added the right connection to reset Podesta's password and then turn 2FA. However, that was not the connection that was clicked; instead, it had been the convincing-looking connection in the first "Someone gets your password" e-mail. The link resulted in a page that seemed to be a standard Google sign-in page.

Nevertheless, it was not (Twitter utilizes the same technique for every single URL posted on its support; which lets it eliminate spam and malicious hyperlinks instantly, by quitting the search along with recognized malicious URLs into the database).

At first glance except that it'd seem as it needs to, and they'd go on and enter a password. From 10.10 a.m., 2FA was turned on to your accounts.

The whole lot was downloaded by them. Also, there were subtle signs the e-mail to Podesta wasn't legitimate. One was at the topic line. "Somebody has you" it appeared to see. However, what looks like the English letter "o" from the words a person' and password' is really an entirely different personality: a Unicode character that resembles an English "o" into an individual reader in most computer fonts—like that used within an iPhone—however, to the pc itself, is not the same in all. (Paradoxically, the distinction is most evident when watching the e-mail about the Wikileaks website, which employs the Courier font and makes the imitation "O" seem like a zero.)

Why use that distinct personality?
The best explanation would be to neutralize Google's spam and anti-virus detection methods, where the term "someone gets your password" coming

out of a non-Google address could be blocked. The Fancy Bear group had likely already experimented with this; and when one odd character had failed, there are a multiplicity of other people to swap to get a new effort at getting past the filters and hooking a sufferer. However, as the hackers were targeting the DNC as well as the campaign group, they also were observed. Bit.ly enables users to set up accounts so they can track click-throughs in their links. However, besides, it lets anybody else monitor just how many have clicked on it, and also what exactly the first URL was, and also what additional URLs that consideration has generated shortened hyperlinks for. SecureWorks managed to pick about connections made by precisely the team out.

The "Someone has your password" component was in white text onto a desperate backdrop; the "CHANGE PASSWORD" connection in text within a box. The design was consistent Although the URL changed. According to an investigation of SecureWorks' study by the Associated Press of 19,000 odd malicious hyperlinks made by Fancy Bear involving October 2015 and May 2016, the initial group was shipped to 10 March targeting heaps of individuals seemingly since they'd worked to the 2008 Clinton effort. The majority of these failed; that does not signify whether credentials were entered, through a number of the hyperlinks have been clicked. In every case, as using the phishing message delivered to Podesta, the first URL was pre-encoded using the e-mail address of the individual being targeted that those details will be filled in on the fake login page. Still another round followed the following day. However, e-mails from the hillaryclinton.com domain used Google's e-mail systems and had 2FA turned, so employees understood a warning about somebody having their password might be dismissed. A number of those efforts frees coming from members of employees, to attempt to make them send passwords or info.

The employees were conscious of their continuing efforts, which they were targeting the DNC. The phishing attempts lasted through March and into May, when scores were targeted in the Clinton campaign and the DNC, although the latter was hacked; analysts guess that there were two classes on the job, with the very same goals but separate surgeries.

The aims for the effort that was spear phishing ranged from employees responsible for travel. However, the safety of the campaign was dominant. Only 20 of those links were clicked; which does not of itself signify they entered their qualifications. Some of the hyperlinks were clicked which may signal to feel than.

Those I spoke to by the campaign team then were adamant: they had been conscious of phishing efforts, and they would not fall to it. 10 Fancy Bear did not confine its phishing to the fundamental group, however. Its selection of e-mails captured several for example one, in groups. Pratt Wiley, the DNC's director of voter defence, was targeted at 15 occasions between March 2016 and October 2015. Among those folks I talked to that worked closely with the effort believed Podesta's account could have been compromised before the March mails; there is no means of knowing whether sooner phishing e-mails were not only taken out of the following data dump. The Clinton campaign could be targeted was not surprising.

There was no one an omission that members of the group felt miserable about. Though there were countless employees. There were four people in the IT facet of the group, none charged with the role. From April 2016, a few from the DNC realized it was murdered, possibly for a while; the FBI was warning it for six months there were hacking efforts underway contrary to its servers. In mid-May, the Clinton campaign staff took a vital step by telling the employees to utilize Signal, an end-to-end encrypted program which delivers text, video and voice calling to Recover telephone numbers. It does not save anything, also resistant to spoofing.

Staff were advised not to discuss anything sensitive through e-mail; somewhat whatever controversial, particularly concerning Donald Trump, needed to undergo Signal. 11 On Friday 10 June that the DNC leadership advised its 100-odd employees to hand into their notebooks. Though they did not say why at that moment, a breach of the DNC's servers was verified by Crowdstrike, which was retained by the company after its suspicions regarding hacking proved too big to ignore. Crowdstrike was convinced that Fancy Bear achieved the hacking, aka APT28, a Russian state-linked team it was observing, and for much more by another team that they called Cozy Bear.

Wikileaks has an excellent year before it... we've got e-mails about Hillary Clinton that area pending book. In retrospect, talked about even the Podesta ones, or the DNC e-mails?

He feared being extradited to the US from Sweden to face trial.

Whatever damage Hillary or her horizons that are restricted was fine by him. About publishing, e-mails and Wikileaks had been concerned. Crowdstrike explained that two Russian classes had broken .13 Over 24 hours, an Internet character referred to as "Guccifer 2.0" delivered a variety of news websites that a little ditch of e-mails and documents, and maintained "that is me who murdered Democratic National Committee." (The choice of title was an intriguing reference: the very first Guccifer was a jobless Romanian cab driver who murdered and dumped the contents of a variety of US and Romanian politicians' e-mails in 2013 and 2014. He whined there in May 2016 and had been extradited to the US. He claimed he had hacked Hillary Clinton server, but provided no evidence. In September that year, he had been detained for just more than four decades.)

Guccifer 2.0 set up a Wordpress site and proclaimed that although Crowdstrike record of "sophisticated hacker classes" breaking to the DNC, it was not that tough, "Guccifer might have been the very first one who uttered Hillary Clinton's and other Democrats' mail servers."

However, he was not the last. Regardless of any hacker might get access to the servers of the DNC "He denied being anything to do with Cozy Bear or even Fancy Bear; he worked and was Romanian he said. He exhibited documents and also promised to have been within the DNC's systems for at least a year, such as an opposition evaluation of the probable strengths and flaws of Donald Trump. The portion of these newspapers, thousands of e-mails and documents, I gave to Wikileaks. They will publish them."

The files were not all accurate, in any case. So suspicions were increased by a few of the facts concerning the hacker. Romanian, as it had been put to him, wasn't understood by him. A number of the metadata revealed it had come through a VPN service. He utilized mounts instead of colons in emoticons common when using the keyboard compared to the Romanian design. The files were opened on servers, along with the metadata revealed settings and titles. There was the usage of a version of Office 2007—popular in Russia.

Everything pointed since the origin to Russian hackers. Would commercial hackers or amateur wish to break in the servers of the DNC?

There was not any money there. The particulars of what happened were arcana.

This made the concept he was different from Fancy Bear. However, also, it revealed strangely some effort employees were using e-mail.

The Smoking Gun attended Clinton reprinted a series of e-mails delivered as employees ready to corral colleagues. E-mails delivered in 10 minutes' back-and-forth seemed bizarre that the dialogue could have been quicker, and will make sense for WhatsApp, texting or even Signal market, unhackable and left traces.

The escape was written up by the Washington Post and remarked that it might "fortify the reality that Clinton prefers to effort in a bubble. She takes questions in the press corps that is travelling." However, there were not leaked e-mails about the effort of Trump. On Friday, in the same way, the Democrats were gathering for their conference Wikileaks released a ditch of 22,000 DNC e-mails, including a number where party members disparaged Bernie Sanders. Sanders fans and the ruler were at one another's throats along with also the DNC chair was made to resign. By then, the effort had moved into a new stage: information warfare.

And, if you don't know about our .xyz site, here are links to back up the aforementioned events/considerations.

Following are public links and resources to support my view on how the Podesta case evolved, you can verify yourself.

We are The Unknowns; Our Knowledge Talks and Wisdom Listens...
MrSecurity

A Cryptography Primer from Club Hell

Club Hell (or "Inferno"), was one of the hacking forums listed on few of the hundreds alternative versions of the Hidden Wiki (the Deep Web version of Wikipedia). Like FreeHacks, one of the largest hacking forums on the Internet, Club Hell used to contain thousands of posts on hacking tutorials, privacy and all sorts of black market onion sites reviews.

One of the posts, called "A cryptography primer," caught my attention and, after starting communication with the anonymous author and the forum administrator, I have got into a IRC chat with the author and got permission to disclose the original post content.

There are several ways to categorize encryption, but for our purposes here, I have broken them down into four main areas.

Symmetric Encryption

Symmetric cryptography is where we have the identical key in the sender and recipient. It's most likely the most common type of cryptography. You've got a password or key which deletes a message, and I have the same password to decrypt the message. Anyone else cannot read our message or information.

Symmetric cryptography is extremely fast, so it's well-suited for bulk storage or streaming software. The disadvantage to symmetric cryptography is called the key exchange. If both ends need the same key, they will need to utilize the third channel to exchange the key and therein lies the weakness. Whether two people wish to reestablish their communication and they're 12,000 miles apart, how can they swap the key? This key exchange afterwards is fraught with all of the issues of the confidentiality of the medium they choose, whether it be phone, mail, e-mail, face-to-face, and so on. The key exchange can be intercepted and leave the confidentiality of the encryption moot. Some of the standard symmetric algorithms That You Need to be familiar with are:

DES—This was one of the original and oldest encryption schemes developed by IBM. It was found to be flawed and breakable and was used in the original hashing system of LANMAN hashes in early (pre-2000) Windows systems.

3DES—This encryption algorithm was developed in response to the flaws in DES. 3DES applies the DES algorithm three times (hence the name "triple DES") making it slightly more secure than DES.

AES—Advanced Encryption Standard is not an encryption algorithm but rather a standard developed by NIST. Presently, it is considered the most robust encryption, uses a 128-, 196-, or 256-bit key and is occupied by the Rijndael algorithm since 2001. Used in WPA2, SSL/TLS, and many other protocols where confidentiality and speed are essential.

RC4—This is streaming (it encrypts each bit or byte rather than a block of information) cypher and developed by Ronald Rivest of RSA fame. Used in VoIP and WEP.

Blowfish—The first of Bruce Schneier's encryption algorithms. It uses a variable key length and is very secure. It is not patented so that anyone can use it without a license.

Twofish—A stronger version of Blowfish using a 128- or 256-bit key and was a strong contender for AES. Used in Cryptcat and Open-PGP, among other places. It also is in the public domain without a patent.

Asymmetric Encryption

Asymmetric cryptography uses different keys on the end of the communication channel. Asymmetric cryptography is extremely slow, about 1,000 times slower than symmetric cryptography; therefore we don't wish to use it for bulk encryption or streaming communication. It will, however, solve the key exchange issue. Since we don't have to have the same key on both ends of communication, we do not have the dilemma of key exchange.

Asymmetric cryptography is used primarily if we have two things unknown to each other that wish to exchange a little bit of data, including a secret or other identifying data, like a certificate. It's not used for streaming or bulk encryption because of its speed limitations.

Some of the common asymmetric encryption schemes you should be familiar with are:

Diffie-Hellman—Many people in the field of cryptography regard the Diffie-Hellman key exchange to be the most significant development in cryptography (I would have to agree). Without going deep into the mathematics, Diffie and Hellman developed a way to generate keys without having to exchange the keys, thereby solving the critical exchange problem that plagues crucial symmetric encryption.

RSA—Rivest, Shamir, and Adleman is a scheme of asymmetric encryption that uses factorization of vast prime numbers as the relationship between the two keys.

PKI—Public essential infrastructure is the widely used asymmetric system for exchanging confidential information using a private key and a public key.

ECC—Elliptical curve cryptography is becoming increasingly popular in mobile computing as it is efficient, requiring less computing power and energy consumption for the same level of security. ECC relies upon the shared relationship of two functions being on the same elliptical curve.

PGP—Pretty Good Privacy uses asymmetric encryption to assure the privacy and integrity of e-mail messages.

Hashes

Hashes are one-way encryption. A password or message is encrypted in a manner it can't be reversed or unencrypted. You may wonder, "What good would it do us to have something encrypted and not have the ability to decrypt it?" Fantastic question! After the message is encrypted it generates a "hash" that becomes a distinctive, but indecipherable signature to the underlying message. Every message is encrypted in a manner that it creates a unique hash. Ordinarily, these hashes are a fixed length (an MD5 hash is always 32 characters). In this way, the attacker can't decipher any information regarding the underlying message in the amount of the hash.

For this reason, we do not need to be aware of the original message; we must find out whether some text generates an identical hash to confirm its integrity. This is the reason why hashes can be used to store passwords. The passwords are stored as hashes and then when someone attempts to log in; the system hashes the password and checks to determine if the hash created matches the hash that's been stored.

Additionally, hashes are helpful for integrity checking, for example with file downloads or program files. In the realm of encryption and hashing, a "crash" is where two separate input texts create the same hash.

To put it differently, the hash isn't unique. This may be an issue once we assume that all of the hashes are unique such as in certification exchanges in SSL. NSA used this land of collisions from the Stuxnet malware to give it what seemed to be a valid Microsoft certificate. Hash algorithms which make collisions, as you might guess, are flawed and insecure.

These are the hashes you should be familiar with.

MD4—This was an old hash by Ron Rivest and has mostly been discontinued in use due to collisions.

MD5—The most widely used hashing system. It's 128-bit and produces a 32-character message digest.

SHA1—Developed by the NSA, it is more secure than MD5. It has
160-bit digest which is usually rendered in 40-character hexadecimal. Usually used for certificate exchanges in SSL, but because of
recently discovered flaws, is being deprecated for that purpose.

Wireless

Wireless cryptography has been a favorite of Null Byte readers as so many
here are trying to crack wireless access points. As you might guess, wireless
cryptography is symmetric (for speed), and as with all symmetric cryptography, key exchange is critical.

WEP—This was the original encryption scheme for wireless and was
quickly discovered to be flawed. It used RC4, but because of the
small key size (24-bit), it repeated the IV about every 5,000 packets
enabling easy cracking on a busy network.

WPA—This was a quick fix for the flaws of WEP, adding a larger key
and TKIP to make it slightly more difficult to crack.

WPA2-PSK—This was the first of the more secure wireless encryption
schemes. It uses a pre-shared key and AES. It then salts the hashes
with the AP name or SSID. The hash is exchanged at authentication
in a four-way handshake between the client and AP.

WPA2-Enterprise—This wireless encryption is one of the most
secure. It uses a 128-bit key, AES, and a remote authentication
server (RADIUS).

In the realm of cryptography, size does matter! Generally speaking, the
bigger the key, the more secure the encryption. This means that AES using
a 256-bit key is stronger than AES having a 128-bit key and probably will
be more challenging to break. Within the same encryption algorithm, the

bigger the key, the stronger the encryption. It doesn't necessarily indicate that bigger keys imply stronger encryption involving encryption algorithms. Between algorithms, the strength of the encryption depends on both the particulars of the algorithm and the critical dimensions.

Encryption algorithms are based on the transformation and permutation of components of information. The classic case of transformation from substitution is the Caesar cypher and its descendant, Vigenere. For instance, we could have the next sentence.

The quick brown fox jumped over the lazy dog.

This sentence can be encrypted with a Caesar cypher with a key of "b"...

VJKS WKEM DTQY PHQZ LWOR GFQX GTVJ KNCB AFQI

Note that the letters have been incremented by two and the formatting removed. Vigenere works similarly, but instead of one letter or number key, it uses several letters and numbers. For example, the same sentence is now encrypted with the keyword "Disney"...

XQXE ZHGT UFTV ROHL OTQY XRTU IAMV JKEI RRTF

We could use a transposition cypher. A transposition cypher doesn't alter the letter's distributions. Instead, it merely scrambles their purchase. A rail fence cypher is among the most famous of the easy transpositions. First, you choose the sentence you would like to encode and write them in staggered formations like this...

t e u c b o n o j m e o e t e a y o
h q i k r w f x u p d v r h l z d g

Then, copy the following row:

TEUC BONO JMEO ETEA YOHQ IKRW FXUP DVRH LZDG

In each case, the sentence is encoded. What if someone wishes to read it enough to try and break it?

Basic Cryptanalysis and Theory

Information isn't the letters nor the collections of pieces. The information is that the patterns these letters and pieces make. Cryptanalysis is all about trying to find patterns that may give clues to what the key is (or what the key is not).

In nature, a cryptanalyst is seeking information from a set of data that's been encrypted, or meta information having to do with the encrypted data. Much of this is from the scope of this guide, but I will likely cover it later.

Before I discuss the concept behind the power of encryption algorithms, I will first use an illustration. Look at my example using the Caesar cypher. Suppose that the attacker (often named Oscar in many cases) understood that the words were encoded using a Caesar cypher. He might attempt to brute force the answer by imagining loads of decryption keys.

"a" uifr vjdl cspx ogpy kvnq fepw fsui fmba zeph
"b" theq uick brow nfox jump edov erth elaz ydog
"c" sgdp thbj aqnv menw itlo dcnu dqsg dkzy xcnf
...

The Caesar cypher is very vulnerable to some brute-force attack as it has a tiny key space. An integral space is the range of possible keys, usually represented by a capital K, subscript l, to denote the number of values a piece' of this key could have, and a superscript n to represent the number of pieces each key. Frequent values for l are 2, 10, and 26. In the event of the Caesar cypher, its key space is K sub 26, which is equivalent to 26. That amount is small enough that Caesar can be brute forced by hand with no computer.

Other methods to gather information regarding the key are to examine patterns in the letters by counting the number of occurrences of individual letters and bigrams. Most languages have basic patterns which are conserved through the encryption procedure. Indeed there are lots of ways to discover patterns, but for this guide, the main thing to consider isn't the how, but how this is true.

Substitution-Permutation Networks

This is among the most popular forms of symmetric block ciphers in use today (Feistel is another). Just as the name says, this sort of cipher uses both substitution and permutation to change the plaintext into cipher-text. To understand how these work, you must first understand that these ciphers first break up the information into chunks. Each chunk is composed of a particular number of bytes called a word. For an example, I will make up a SPN that has a substitution section, a permutation section, and a whitening segment. Suppose I have the hexadecimal code:0xa258fe1bIf I defined my word size to be 4 pieces (1/2 byte), then I could divide it up like this...

a 2 5 8 f e 1 b

For the substitution stage, I will add three to everyone...

D 5 8 B 2 4 E

Then I will permute the information by transferring each word two to the right and then shifting the next word with the third, the fourth with the fifth, and so on until the eighth is switched with the first.

1 D E 8 2 B 4

Ultimately, I will take my key (0x01234567) and I will XOR it to the current data. This practice is called whitening.

1 C C 6 1 7 D 3

This may look like the result, but it's not! No.

In the modern SPNs, we would do this several days before we were done.

Rijndael, aka AES, uses a more complex set of substitutions and per-mutations, adds in a key generator that generates a key for each cycle and repeats the process 12 times! These processes are sufficiently complex and arbitrary that any change in the key or the plaintext will impact each and every bit in the block.

Encryption cannot do everything for you. There are a lot of things it can do though. By way of example, encryption can be used to keep you messages safe, obviously.

With a sufficiently strong encryption scheme and a sufficiently strong key, even a government can't break encryption.

Cryptography is used daily, hourly, secondly (my English teacher be damned!) for online transactions. You're aware that your credit card number is sent every time you shop at a new site, right? Without public-key cryptography, we couldn't shop online with any semblance of security. Cryptography can also be used for file integrity assurance. Using hashes, we can be sure that because the last time a file was "hashed," the file hasn't been altered. Finally, using hashes and signature schemes, we can confirm a person's identity with no meeting them. However encryption cannot do everything.

As I said, a sufficiently good encryption scheme can't be broken even by a government. However, if the government in question is really that interested in your information, they can only make you give them the password using whatever means are available to them.

This brings me to my second point. Encryption does not guarantee secrecy of communication, only of the content. In fact, the fact that something is encrypted is so apparent that a strong entity can use it to tag your communication across the Internet.

This practice is called traffic analysis and is, once more, outside the scope of this article. If you would like to avoid traffic analysis, you want to obfuscate the endpoint with proxies (such as a TOR route), or you need to conceal the fact that your communicating secretly with steganography.

A Conversation with A1d3n

This is the raw paste of the chat with A1d3n following a post reply on the dark web network Atlayo.

Hello,
A1d3n here, I found your post on Atlayo interesting, so I decided to send a message. :P

My name is A1d3n, I've been a regular on dark web for over two years (probably five years of actually using Tor), and I guess you could say I'm a privacy "hacktivist." I'm pretty experienced on staying anonymous, keeping a secure setup, and basic programming/scripts. I only use Linux and

I'm in college studying cyber security. I'm probably more gray hat though, so I don't try to screw people over, heh.

I've seen a lot of different kinds of people on the dark web, and I'd love to answer any questions you have. :)

Also, I'm not doing this for a donation and if you don't want to donate, you don't have to. But if you do, my BTC address is:

1EHvDo6Jepe7jNgMbCrtRcJbxgvXo27dsZ

If you're interested, please lemme know. I'm excited to hear your questions. :) Any opportunity I have to promote privacy, security, and peace of mind, I'll happily take it. ^_^

I'm also a moderator on several chats, including:
Daniel's Chat: http://danschatjr7qbwip.onion/chat.php
Evil Chat: http://evilchatxp24s7vb.onion/chat.php
ChatBox: http://chatboxdb7vifffz.onion/

I'm also a half-op on MadIRC: qj3m7wxqk4pfqwob.onion
Finally, my website is: http://A1d3nm7chl2xypu4.onion/
What's your book? I'd love to read it!!

Respectfully,
~A1d3n

———

Hi A1d3n,
Sure, let's start with defining the topic(s) of our conversation over e-mail. Would you feel comfortable about talking on topics such as challenges you currently experience working as moderator for DW chats/IRCs and also give few details on what are you preferences in relation to privacy and communication in the DW? Do you think AES is ok or 3DES should be the way to go for super secure communications? (even 3DES is very resource demanding). Complex algorithms versus long Keys, any preferences? Since privacy is a big topic on the DW, what is the level of understanding on the security designs you see in the DW when working with chats?

Thank you

Hey,

Thanks for the quick reply. :)

> Would you feel comfortable about talking on topics such as challenges you currently experience working as moderator for DW chats/IRCs and also give few details on what are you preferences in relation to privacy and communication in the DW?

Sure, some challenges I face with DW chats is actually just dealing with drama in such a small community. Other than that, there's the occasional spammer (which sometimes requires the group to be set to members-only) or someone posts illegal content, so the message has to be removed and the poster kicked. Since everyone is anonymous, you can't simply IP-ban someone, but you can still take various measures to enforce the rules. The chats I moderate don't allow extreme or illegal content (at least in most countries), but what people do in private encrypted messages is none of my business.

When it comes to privacy and security on the DW, I believe everyone should be as secure as possible and trust no one. Privacy is a right, just like many companies say (including Apple). I'm no Apple fanboy, but that's one thing I like about them. If it were up to me, everyone would be using end-to-end encryption that supports perfect forward secrecy and deniability. However, this is obviously not the case with most people on most platforms, and I think this should be changed.

Do you think AES is ok or 3DES should be the way to go for super secure communications?

Between the 2, I'm gonna have to go with AES on this one (AES256 specifically), since it uses stronger encryption keys and is faster to encrypt. 3DES is really just an adaptation of DES, while AES is totally different. AES also became a federal government standard for encryption and I use it for tons of stuff. When it comes to complex algorithms versus long keys, it really depends... By complex, if you mean "easy to compute but hard to reverse," then I would say: complexity is very important, but key length, while it plays a roll, is not always the defining factor.

> Since privacy is a big topic on the DW, what is the level of understanding on the security designs you see in the DW when working with chats?

When it comes to PHP-based chats, I assume all conversations are compromised/public. With IRCs, your connection can be secure, but as the documentation on whonix.org suggests, these are considered public arenas. Only when one is using a one-on-one OTR conversation (Off-The-Record plugin for XMPP clients) or the experimental OMEMO plugin for multi-user chat can one begin to assume their conversations are safe. Also, these types of technologies have to be used correctly and not half-assed.

Tech stuff aside, I've found that people on the dark web are usually more intelligent, technologically savvy, and even nicer! When it comes to the privacy policies of many websites and companies such as Google, I feel more comfortable and even happier here where data is anonymized and people can be free of being tracked in an ever tech-reliant world.

These are my thoughts on things and I hope I've answered your questions satisfactorily. :)

Sincerely,
~A1d3n

Hi A1d3n,
Here are more questions for you, feel free to take your time to reply:

- Google, Twitter, Apple and several other technology companies have recently updated their terms and conditions;
  Facebook, for example, has updated its data policy in an
  effort to allay users' privacy concerns. Entire YT channels and
  social media pages of public figures involved with debates
  related to politics, society and human rights have been taken
  down, causing large debates among large groups of freedom
  and privacy advocates both online and offline. Do you think
  this might spark interest or curiosity among the clearnet
  community on deep web hosting? Do you see a future where

journalists or public figures uses onion websites to host their controversial contents?

1. What are your concerns about DW hosting? I have previously interviewed one person involved with Deep Web hosting that offers site hosting "over I2P and Tor for increased security and anonymity." What is your take on DW hosting and what you think should be a big improvement for a end user interested in host his/her website on the DW?
2. DeepPeep, Intute, Deep Web Technologies, Torch, NotEvil, and Ahmia.fi are a few search engines that have accessed the deep web. The UCLA created a hidden-Web crawler that automatically generated meaningful queries to issue against search forms and the Stanford Computer Science Department, Stanford University has presented an architectural model for a hidden-Web crawler that used key terms provided by users or collected from the query interfaces to query a Web form and crawl the Deep Web content. Which one is your favorite DW search engine and, in your opinion, are Sitemap Protocol and The Open Archives Initiative Protocol for Metadata Harvesting (OAI-PMH) valid improvements to allow search engines to discover DW resources?
3. What is your take on Penetration Testing Linux distributions such as Kali, BlackArch or ParrotSec?
4. Do you support/use compartmentalized OS like Qubes?
5. Can you share a technology relevant story related to your current involvement with DW chats /IRCs?

Thank you

Hey,

Google, Twitter, Apple and several other technology companies have recently updated their terms and conditions

This is a start, and I'm glad it was done. I'm just the type of guy that's very skeptical of non-FOSS software and I don't agree with the idea of targeted ads. Who knows what this information about you may be used for, despite these new "safeguards" in place?

Do you think this might spark interest or curiosity among the clearnet community on deep web hosting?

Yes, as long as the word gets out there. I personally don't agree with people like Alex Jones, but I support his right to say it. Most people I've talked to on here agree with me and are very against censorship.

Do you see a future where journalists or public figures uses onion websites to host their controversial contents?

This is already done on small scales, so I've heard. Obviously it hasn't blown up yet, but I do see a future in it; either Tor or I2P. Brave Browser, for instance, now comes with Tor-powered tabs, making dark web browsing much easier for the layman.

Brave advances browser privacy with Tor-powered tabs: https://cnet.com/news/brave-advances-browser-privacy-with-tor-powered-tabs/

What is your take on DW hosting and what you think should be a big improvement for a end user interested in host his/her website on the DW?

For someone setting up their own Tor hidden service, essentially, all they must do is set up a web server and modify the torrc file to point to the website data, using SQL if necessary. When you say "big improvement," are you referring to usability or security? For usability, concise documentation should be more readily available. When it comes to security, if you are not confident in using your own home server, you can rent a VPS (connecting via ssh through Tor) or use a hosting service. I'm not sure how this could really be "improved" if you are doing the hosting yourself, other than simply improving your own technical abilities. All the tools are there to pull it off just fine, so good documentation goes a long way.

A VPS, or virtual private server, is beneficial, because if your server becomes compromised, it shouldn't be traced back to you (as long as proper security practices were taken when accessing it).

Which one is your favorite DW search engine and, in your opinion, are Sitemap Protocol and The OAI-PMH valid improvements to allow search engines to discover DW resources?

I've had a lot of luck with Ahmia, but more luck by using .onion directories:

Fresh Onions: http://zlal32teyptf4tvi.onion/
DeepLink: http://deeplinkdeatbml7.onion/index.php
Daniel's Link List: http://onionsnjajzkhm5g.onion/onions.php
Some have great advanced search options and Daniel Winzen's onion
 link list script is very good.
GitHub link: https://github.com/DanWin/onion-link-list

I actually think these are pretty good improvements to discovering darknets, in addition to DARPA's Memex search tool. Web hosters simply need to be aware of what's in their robots.txt file and act accordingly. There may be some privacy concerns over this and MAY be used for correlation attacks, so I'll definitely be looking more into it. It's a hard trade-off to make; I don't want Tor to stop being anonymous (more darknets will appear), but at the same time, there are some disgusting sites/services out there I'd wish could be taken down.

What is your take on Penetration Testing Linux distributions such as Kali, BlackArch or ParrotSec?

My take is that these are very specialized operating systems designed to be used by a skilled pentester who understands how to use the tools. I have seen many, many cases where someone with almost no Linux experience downloads Kali, thinking it will make him/her a hacker. Obviously, this isn't the case, since the (mostly command-line) tools require some knowledge before use. Clearly, you can install nearly the same tools on Arch or a basic debian install, but the benefit of something like Kali (especially a live boot) is the fact that everything comes pre-installed and is ready to be used in an attack (whether for good or bad).

Do you support/use compartmentalized OS like Qubes?

Absolutely. I've used it myself and I think it's a great solution to many of today's security concerns. I've never seen an OS that's so secure, yet so easy to use. As Micah Lee from the Freedom of the Press Foundation once said, it really makes you feel like a god. With Qubes, you're in control of the software; not the other way around!

Can you share a technology relevant story related to your current involvement with DW chats /IRCs?

This may come across as obvious to some tech savvy people and web developers, but there was recently an issue where screenshots were being faked on a PHP-based chat. It turns out it's entirely easy to right click, inspect element, alter a message, and then take a screenshot. Simple things like this can cause deep confusion in some people, so it's always important to keep in mind the security structure of the chat you're talking on and know when to take it with a grain of salt.

From my perspective, only an encrypted and signed message can truly be trusted, and even then, only to a reasonable degree (as opposed to absolute 100 percent trust). Just like the Qubes philosophy says, we should all "distrust the infrastructure" whenever our data is not fully in our control. This doesn't mean don't use things like CloudFlare, but having a signed website repo that can be cloned and its signatures verified is a good start.

Please let me know if you have any more questions. I would just like to clarify: My name is A1d3n with an E, not an A. Thanks! :)

Sincerely,
~A1d3n

Hey,

It was a pleasure ^_^

Had you ever encountered directly (either via Chat, IRC or forums) with groups of hacktivists/activists?

I have encountered a few activists, including ones from China and Iran. I've also chatted with several people from Russia as well, who are usually easy to spot. Recently, I met someone from Africa who is desperately trying to make money and is dedicated to learning how to hack (and making significant progress too). Many of these people do complain about censorship and corrupt governments, which draws them here. Conversations with them are usually interesting, but unfortunately there isn't much I can do to help them besides guide them in the right direction. As far as activist "groups," I can't say I've seen many, nor do I seek them out. I have seen a few advertisements for hacker groups, though.

In your opinion, what are some of the key features to improve technologies already existing in the DW such as search engines, hosting and communication in general?

What I don't want to see is a powerful, centralized search engine for the dark web with tons of algorithms and tracking features. What I do want to see is an improved directory system that makes it easier to search for keywords, but doesn't mine the data to look for patterns and correlations. A company like Google does a wonderful job of providing a usable search engine, but I choose to use Startpage or DuckDuckGo because privacy is more important to me than ever-so-slightly better search results. Obviously, Google is not the only one who does this, but they are certainly one of the biggest. I've noticed the "fight or flight" response is sort of non-existent when it comes to the cyber world (often due to users' unawareness or lack of understanding of technology), but if the thought "I wonder what they do with my data" ever crosses your mind, then it's worth looking into if you ask me.

When it comes to hosting, I think there should be more free hosting services. I know a couple people who were thinking about doing this, myself included. I don't have a lot of money at the moment as a poor college student, but when I do, I think this is a nice way of giving back to this community. This will make it easier for people to host their own hidden service without much administrative overhead or requiring too much experience. Of course, there would be certain types of content I wouldn't allow (such as child abuse or zoophilia), but for the most part it would be completely uncensored.

Communication is not currently an issue in my eyes. It's not difficult to communicate and find secure ways to do so. The more we educate people on the importance of encryption and authentication, the safer everyone will be. I like Tor because it takes you back in time to the earlier days of the Internet with less automation, less javascript, and more simplicity. It's like an old school, yet futuristic breath of fresh air away from the chaos of the clearnet, and I hope it stays that way.

Thanks for the interesting questions, some of which really made me think. No one has asked me that activist question before, so that was pretty cool. Please let me know if you'd like me to clarify any of my answers, and I can't wait to see your book! :)

Sincerely,

~A1d3n

Hey,

Yeah, I'm up for that. What do you think about the use of bridges or a VPN to hide the usage of Tor? I think one can argue it's better to use Tor directly with a social approach. The more people that use Tor, the more anonymous Tor users will be. Your thoughts?

~A1d3n

By the way, when I decrypt your messages, I get this:

gpg: WARNING: message was not integrity protected

Hi A1d3n,

Yes, the "gpg: WARNING: message was not integrity protected," it's because I should use a stronger AES-256, but since I will have to reveal my identity anyway (you will see from the book) I am not too picky with my PGP.

The more people that use Tor, the more anonymous Tor users will be. Your thoughts?

Definitely, the more people who run Tor as a relay or a bridge, the faster and safer the network becomes... I know that in 2017 the Tor project started featuring new algorithms and improved authentication schemes. Also, introduction of sandboxing, allowing Tor network processes to be separated from rest of a user's computer, and the adoption of the Kernel Informed Socket Transport (KIST) algorithm to lower latency for users that use Tor for regular web browsing are all signs that Tor is pushing in the direction of mainstream usage. On another note, the ooni-probe distribution for Raspberry Pis (https://ooni.torproject.org/install/lepidopter/) is a cool project by Tor to show their involvement in open source hardware too.

I still think that adoption of Tor on large scale will require education, tutorials and more awareness for non-technical users on topics like privacy and freedom of speech. Also getting schools or local groups involved with collaborative education projects for small group of students (for ex. setup relays) would definitely be a good way to increase awareness.

What are your thoughts?

Hey,

Yeah, everyone should run a relay and/or bridge! Security by isolation is definitely something that should be implemented more. I didn't know about the KIST algorithm and the ooniprobe project, so that's really cool. It's great to see stuff like that being made to expand the avenues of the Tor project.

Adapting Tor on a large scale will be no easy task, in my opinion. Whenever I meet new users on Tor, they often come with preconceived notions about what the place is like. Often they come from the land of YouTube, which is full of "creepypastas" about the dark web (usually involving hit men and red rooms), and they buy into a lot of the myths. I agree that proper education on this and other anonymous networks such as I2P would really help people understand it better. I really think it's only a matter of time before people start forming those kinds of collaborative groups, setting up relays, and hosting their own sites/services.

Every single day there's tons of people who use Tor for the first time, so it's worth at least making the information more available and accessible to everyone. Some will argue that the Tor Project's website already has all the information you could possibly need, but I'd argue: the more the better! What do you think?

~A1d3n

Hey,

A1d3n is fine. :)

That's an interesting view on the online world. By your definition, I'm more of a "deep web" user, as opposed to using "dark" illicit services somewhere. I think as more people become technologically savvy, the more people will, at the very least, know that Tor exists and the basics of it. I still meet tons of people every day who've never even heard of it.

My experience as a chat moderator is probably a little different than most, but then again, we're all unique in our own way. I didn't even plan on becoming a moderator/half-operator; it just kind of happened. When a group of people get together in a chat room, someone's got to make sure the rules are followed. There are some clear technical differences between a PHP chat (such as Daniel's) and an IRC. If someone breaks the rules in an IRC, we can kick the user or set a ban on their nick, but we can't erase the message. To get around this, only "voiced" users can send links in the IRC I use, which prevents guests from sharing disgusting sites or doxxes. With a PHP-based chat, messages can be deleted, but the chat is much slower than an IRC (refreshes every 10 seconds). In fact, they aren't ideal without javascript, at least from my experience. Since a lot of Tor users turn off javascript (myself included), it really narrows it down to IRCs or non-JS webchats.

Technical stuff aside, as a moderator it helps to treat everyone equally (yes, even guests) and give people the benefit of the doubt without being too naive. Just treat everyone like a person and usually things will work out. :)

Hopefully, this has interested you in some shape or form. There's not a whole lot of work when it comes to moderating as long as you enforce the rules, keep people safe, and be nice to people. My favorite thing is actually just helping new people who want to boost their privacy, install Linux, or just have some questions. When in doubt, Google/DuckDuckGo is your friend.

And thank you for your time as well!

Sincerely,
~A1d3n

‐‐‐‐‐‐

Hey,
I have seen somewhat of a trend of using more mobile devices for these types of "dark" activities. I can see the advantage of people who need to be

out on the field to be able to receive encrypted messages, but in general, I think this is a bad idea. I see a mobile phone as a surveillance device. I assume I'm always being tracked wherever I go, and the built-in camera and microphone always active. Unless you physically remove them from the device, how do you know they aren't being used? Also, it's not like you can install something like Qubes or Whonix onto a mobile phone, so I think they should be used sparingly. Phones can still be secure, but the fact that we bring them everywhere is a big enough red flag for me. Also, I'd suggest not backing up to iCloud/Google. It's clear that Apple/Google don't actually delete all types of data immediately after you do. A proper warrant can recover recently deleted data, or even just a very clever social engineer. After the San Bernadino attacks, the FBI was able to access all iCloud data, but since the terrorist didn't back up anything, they had to unlock the phone instead. I'm glad they were able to find more information on him in order to possibly arrest others, but at the same time, Cellebrite also sells its services to tyrannical governments to unlock the phones of peaceful dissidents or activists.

My opinion is: Never put something illegal in electronic form, but if you DO, then don't use a multi-purpose GPS-enabled device that you carry in your pocket 24/7 and is backed up on someone else's servers.

That being said, Telegram's Super Secret Chats are extremely secure, despite not being fully open-source. It's the not-as-encrypted groups that get people in trouble. I haven't heard of Net-Net but I'll be sure to look into it. Another good option is Signal, which has a similar encryption rating as Telegram's Super Secret Chats.

For cryptocurrency, I believe it's best to have either a hardware wallet or something like Electrum stored in a virtual machine with an offline encrypted backup. The passphrase should be stored in a secure but reliable manner. I knew someone that lost over 10k because he stored his passphrase in KeyPass, and the KeyPass backup was corrupted. Yeah, a fun day for sure.

For the normal user, it's kind of silly to say "never use a phone," but at the very least it's important to look through the privacy settings once in a while. I use an iPhone and I can trust it to a reasonable degree, but I still assume it's a listening device, and there's no way I'd use it for anything other than "clearnet" activities!

When it comes to using mobile phones, do you see the same downsides that I do? If so, is there a good solution to it?

Sincerely,
A1d3n

ICS

A Brief History of Industrial Computer Systems Malware

2010: Stuxnet

> *Analyzing the professional activities of the first organizations to fall victim to Stuxnet gives us a better understanding of how the whole operation was planned. At the end of the day this is an example of a supply-chain attack vector, where the malware is delivered to the target organization indirectly via networks of partners that the target organization may work with.*
>
> —Alexander Gostev (Kaspersky Lab)

Kaspersky Lab found Foolad Technic Engineering Co., Beh Pajooh Co. Elec and Comp. Engineering, Neda Industrial Group, Control-Gostar Jahed Company and Kala Electric (Kalaye Electric Co.) among the organizations identified after examining more than 2,000 Stuxnet files collected over a two-year period.

Stuxnet was the first malware to specifically target SCADA systems and programmable logic controllers (PLCs). The main responsible for Iran's nuclear program sabotage, and probably the best example "where the malware is delivered to the target organization indirectly via networks of partners that the target organization may work with."

Kaspersky Lab's Global Research and Analysis Team (GReAT) labeled Stuxnet as the digital equivalent of the atomic attacks on Nagasaki and Hiroshima. Due to design flaws and bugs, Stuxnet ended up behaving like a virus and propagate over the Internet infecting over one hundred thousand systems on top of the systems initially designated as part of the attack.

The origins of Stuxnet have been the subject of speculation since it started to get media coverage in Spring 2010.

According to a New York Times article released during 2012, anonymous sources are quoted as saying that Western governments have taken part in facilitating a cyber-attack against Iran. The effort involved the National Security Agency (NSA) and an undisclosed Israeli military unit known as Unit 8200, The New York Times reported.

Primarily designed to compromise software used at nuclear facilities to control data acquisition, Stuxnet targets frequency converters. Stuxnet target is to sabotage the control of systems in charge of power supplied to motors.

Stuxnet used zero-day vulnerabilities targeting Microsoft products to infect computers.

2013: Havex

The Havex remote access tool (or RAT for short) has been linked to the Russian group known as "Energetic Bear." Identified in spring 2014 after a series of attacks aimed at industrial control systems covered by security firm F-Secure, the Havex RAT family was already featured in the 2013 Global Threat Report by cybersecurity firm CrowdStrike.

Trojanized software was being planted on ICS/SCADA hacked vendor websites: a total of more than 80 variants of the RAT and 140 plus command and control servers (C&C) have been identified as responsible for illegal data acquisition operations.

F-Secure has analyzed the Havex components and find out the standards that provide linked bridge for Windows-based software to collect data and sensitive information on compromised devices and send it back to C&C servers via Object Linking and Embedding (OLE) for Process Control (OPC).

Havex can be described as a family of remote access trojans used for espionage campaigns targeting ICS environments. If first scans for SCADA or ICS devices on compromised networks, and forward information back to the attacker. The core mission of the Haex intelligence extraction tool is not to disrupt or damage an industrial system.

2014: BlackEnergy

The BlackEnergy malware is crimeware turned APT tool and is used in significant geopolitical operations lightly documented over the past year.
                —Kurt Baumgartner and Maria Garnaeva (Kaspersky Lab)

Anomalies detected during 2013 in the BlackEnergy configuration files, lead to unusual activity on one of the BlackEnergy CnC (command-and-control) servers. At first, BlackEnergy's plugins were used to run distributed denial-of-service attacks (DDoS). The Sandworm team was one of the earlier adopters of the Malware, the same Malware later on adopted in several geopolitical operations involving APT tools.

A series of studies have led to the conclusion that Sandworm might keep their non-Windows hacker tools in separate servers and folders to protect their servers.

Some of the WIndows plugins include:

"Fs"—searches for given file types
"Rd"—remote desktop access
"Dstr"—overwrites hard drives with random data until they become
    unusable

After collecting plugins over an extended period, researchers have linked the attacks to Russia, Poland and Ukraine among other countries.

2014–2015: BlackEnergy 2

A variant of the already existing malware BlackEnergy, BlackEnergy 2 was designed to target HMI software (human-machine interfaces) from General Electric, Siemens, Advantech/Broadwin and several other vendors. BlackEnergy 2 is infamously known for the 2015 attack that took down the Ukrainian power grid.

2016: Industroyer/Crash Override

Known for the winter 2016 attack on transmission substations in Ukraine, Crash Override is the best-known Malware designed explicitly for electric grid systems attacks. Initially discovered by ESET (which renamed it "Industroyer"), the malware has been a matter of study by company Dragos Inc., which tracks it as CrashOverride. Industroyer is only the fourth known Malware designed to target industrial control systems. Other ICS related Malware families such as Stuxnet Havex and BlackEnergy seem to have links to CrashOverride: even there are no code similarities between the malware, ELECTRUM actor (linked to CrashOverride usage) seem to have ties to the BlackEnergy group named Sandworm and the malware components share similar concepts.

A real-life scenario would involve coordinated attacks on multiple sites running an infinite loop where breakers open and close until protections are triggered, or the substation goes offline.

Industroyer/CrashOverride is made of several components:

- A backdoor that allows the attackers to execute commands on the compromised systems. It would initiate a time-based communication over the Tor network via command and control (C&C) servers.
- A launcher.
- A data wiper that involves clearing registry keys, and overwriting ICS configuration and Windows files, to help the attackers hide their tracks and make it more challenging to restore damage systems.
- Various payloads which allow attackers to control circuit breaker, and other tools like custom-built port scanners and a denial-of-service (DoS) tools which take advantage of the Siemens Patches Vulnerabilities in SIPROTEC, SIMATIC or similar vulnerabilities.

The in-depth understanding of the technology behind used in the energy sector suggests that some of the malware's developers might have ties or previously worked for companies involved in running power grid operations and industrial network communications.

2017: Triton

The TRITON family is compromised of main modules trilog.exe (Main executable leveraging libraries.zip) and library.zip (custom communication library for interaction with Triconex controllers). The TRITON can be used to modify application memory on Triconex Safety Instrumented System (SIS, the autonomous control system that independently monitors the status of processes) controllers, which prevents controllers from functioning correctly, increasing the chances of failure.

Some of the real-life scenarios include the use of the SIS itself to shut down a process (for example, by triggering a false positive), reprogram the SIS (redesign the logic to allow unsafe conditions are impacting equipment and human safety) and use the Distributed Control System to create a hazard.

How an ICS malware attacks.

- A remote connection may be used to infiltrate the industrial network
- Once inside the network, the adversary can scan the network to identify ICS devices
- Since ICS networks do not use authentication or encryption, an adversary can access any system—including operator or engineering workstations, HMIs, Windows Servers, or controllers (PLC, RTU or DCS controller)—to identify assets to target in the attack
- The attacker extracts information gathered via reconnaissance to an off-site location. This could be accomplished by passing the information internally from different systems to a single location from which it can be extracted.
- Malware is installed on a workstation with access to the targeted ICS system(s) using knowledge gathered in steps one and two, mentioned earlier. This can be accomplished via the network, or by using an infected USB drive.
- The malware replaces existing logic and uploads new ladder logic to the controller (PLC, RTU or DCS controller). Since this logic determines how automated processes are executed, changing or replacing it with malicious payloads can result

from a wide range of operational disruptions and even physical damage to systems, the environment and humans.

ICS Facts Versus Myth

with Robert M. Lee

Robert is the CEO and founder of his own company, Dragos, Inc., that provides cyber security solutions for industrial control system networks. Consider the 2015 attack on the Ukraine power grid when for the first time in history a power grid went down due to an intentional cyberattack. He joined the United States Air Force and became a cyberspace warfare operations officer in the U.S. intelligence community. In that role, he created and led a mission examining nation-states targeting ICS, the first mission of its kind in the U.S. intelligence community. Robert has a master's degree in cybersecurity and computer forensics from Utica College as well as cyber and warfare training through the U.S. Air Force, and he's pursuing his doctorate in war studies from King's College London. He was named one of Forbes' 30 under 30 in Enterprise Technology in 2016, was awarded Energy Sec's 2015 Cyber Security Professional of the Year and named one of Passcode's "Influencers."

The following is an edited transcript from notes taken during Robert E. Lee lecture at "Cybersecurity With The Best" conference and a phone call interview during early 2018.

"There have been many discussions lately on ICS or industrial control systems the type of systems that operate things like the power grid and water filtration and oil and gas pipelines. Also, we have seen a rise in intrusions that are given many people a good bit of alarm. So we want to make sure that we have an excellent presentation on exactly what we can and what we shouldn't be concerned with. Also, a little bit of the nuance that sometimes gets lost.

I run a firm called Dragos, Inc., an industrial security firm. I am also a course author and instructor with the SANS Institute where I authored the community's ICS instant response and course as well as the threat intelligence course for the larger broader inverse infosec community. Also, the previous life I spent time in the U.S. government and while over in one of the intelligence agencies I built their first mission looking at the Nation States breaking into industrial security sites are shooting industrial sites. So a career looking at these threats I'm for pushing my career was also on the offense as well for the government. So I try to bring a little bit of perspective on what it's like to be an offensive person as well as that defender and intelligence analyst. They often find that folks on one side of the fence tend to think everybody else's job is more straight-forward. There's quite a bit of nuance there that need to be captured so we can understand and prepare correctly. So my agenda is pretty simple over this next 30 minutes we're going to first dive into the fiction some the hype around reporting. I often joke around that there's no good news story about the power.

Sometimes we hear some excellent reporting like after major events like Hurricane Harvey and Irma it was newsworthy just how fast those operators and grid workers got back and got the power back in those regions. That was cool, but frequently it's the headlines like oh my gosh we're all going to die. Power grids failure to build a bunker. Also, that's not reasonable. Also, then we'll jump into ICS facts, and I'll walk you through sort of how attacks exist and work. So I will end it on a case study with what happened in Ukraine.

I also write a little comics I found in my time in the military and the government that being able to condense things down to three pain. The comics were pretty effective at communicating technical topics to generals and members of Congress and the like. I still do that over a little Bobby comic every Sunday.

However, here we have the CSO waxing poetically that they need to ensure that there are no attacks that occur. Little Bobby asked for a security budget the CSO tells them I would cut it all out and little Bobby rightfully says Well then I can assure you we'll never see any attacks. So that's also what kind of leads to this hype and reporting where there's not much information that gets shared around real attacks and real cases and real incidents. Also, it's pretty standard that this subject matter is essential everybody. Many people are interested in the power grid oil refineries manufacturing sites units. It's an exciting topic for many folks. What ultimately happens is as there is not much information shared. People worry and fear the worst. It's very common in DC.

I'm based in Maryland I routinely run across congressional staffers and folks many who are trying to do excellent work but sometimes they have the idea that because we don't get visibility into the threats that are targeting industrial that it must be worse than we that we fear worse than we can imagine. Also, that's not necessarily the case. I often tell people that the threats are worse than we realize but they're not as bad as we can imagine. So there are things that go on. However, of course in the lack of that information that's where that's where the hype forms. People want to tell a story but of course not being backed by facts. So let's walk through a couple of these the early ones in the community happened. I mean he's been around forever wild stories. However, the early ones are in Illinois there was a water utility Colonel Gardner, and it's had a pump failure under the state regulations that neither reported the pump failure. The fusion centre for the state got to report that there was a pump failure at the site but 2011 was just the year after most people learned that state it was a thing. Right so in 2010 when Stuxnet and I were like oh my gosh I see us skate. It's everywhere, and then people sort of dawning on that yeah industrial systems are everywhere. There was much concern that there was some cyber attack back in the United States. Also, that would be a pump failure in a water utility which I joked at the time that if you know, the Russians or the Iranians or anybody was going to target the US if their significant effect was having a pump failing and a small utility that night I think broke.

At the time the Staples Center folks got involved.

It ended up getting looked at, and they didn't correctly talk to the engineers or the folks on the ground, and they were getting access to the logs and saw that there was a Russian IP address in the logs five months before the pump failure. So they made a correlation kind of error and said Aha. Because there was a Russian IP in the logs. We know that the Russians were emoting in and therefore they caused the failure.

First of all, of course, we don't do attribution based off of IP address lookups.

Second of all just because something occurred on the network doesn't necessarily mean that was related to the outage or the failure. So in fact, this would get leaked, and it got leaked out to the news media and the news media ran the story Russian cyber attack on water utility the contractor who did the remote thing and read it in the papers and said Well hold on. That told me what it was a contract was on vacation in St. Petersburg and remote it into the utility, and that's why the Russian IP showed up, and the pump only failed because there was just a buildup of residues and that build up caused a failure that was pretty typical and pretty normal to occur in many people got hyped up pretty quickly about this. Another big one as well. The Norse ran cyber attacks. I remember this when it first came out I was still in the government the time I didn't leave the intelligence community and military until 2015. However, in the beginning, portions of 2013 transitioned out. I remember getting a call 3:00 O'clock in the morning.

Like sure they're going nowhere but I can get into an office does this line not secure. I can find the classified line.

However, who is this? Oh, this is so-and-so in the National Security Council, and they don't need to tell you much about military ranks in the government to let you know that Captain Lee was pretty far under where the National City Council could have been contacting. I guess they read my name on some of the ICS reporting that was being done in the government and somebody freaked out wanted to get some ground truth on what was happening. This genuinely green document from a vendor called "x" that said Iran is preparing for a cyber offensive. They are getting ready to attack a bunch of industrial control systems in the United States. Also, they said that they had already attacked five hundred thousand times which should give you some level of understanding that the metrics don't match reality. So as you read through the report, it was pretty apparent that what they were talking about as they stood up honey-pots on the Internet and sometimes even possible just IP ranges for every single scan from an Iranian IP address they registered as one. Also, if it had anything to do with like Port 5 0 2 or port one or two or any of these DDD ports that had anything to do with ICS they registered that as an ICS cyber attack completely inappropriate.

We were able to push back on that pretty quickly on the government channels, but unfortunately, they took it and partner with the conservative think tank AEI and tried to re-release it. In April 2015 they said look based on the Norse cyber attack data nuclear negotiations with Iran should fail because we have proof that if you relieve Iranian sanctions, they will use this relief to target industrial control systems and critical infrastructure. I thought this was highly inappropriate over the carrier based politics about the Iran situation. However, I would hope that we can all agree that political decisions, especially between states, should probably be built off of real data may be even real threat intelligence not no honeypot scans of non-ICS. That was an excellent example of our community getting inappropriately thrown into politics. Also, then, of course, we had another one 2008 Turkey pipeline explosion, so in 2008 a pipeline called the BTC pipeline in Turkey did explode fireball. Luckily everyone that I'm familiar with some everyone I know if I feel safe in that case which is excellent. Years later about six years later Bloomberg ended up publishing a report saying hey that mysterious Oh pipeline was a Russian cyber attack. So that was at odds with what we knew from historical purposes because at the time that it occurred back in 2008 the Turkish government said it was the Kurdish extremists and the Kurdish extremists came out and said Yeah it was us.

It was pretty proper attribution at the time so to hear that there was a new theory being waged and that was a cyber attack and by Russia was pretty intense. So, I got involved in talking to journalists and trying to do our digging. Moreover, as it turns out I don't, I don't think the journalist meant to mislead anybody. Also, I don't think anything was intentionally wrong on their part. I think that it was a complex, nuanced technical topic. I mean I think they got misled by some responders. What ultimately happened is after the attack some innocent responders went into the control centre and they found malware beginning out to a Russian IP address and just like the first you know Colonel Gardner case that we talked about where people assigned to an inappropriate causal analysis is the responders determined. Aha. Because there was an explosion and because there was malware on the controls centre they must be related. So again that's not true. So actually, there were tons of information historical and leaked information about precisely what happened to the BTC pipeline.

They even found explosives and various fractures on the pipeline caused by some physical presence of people.

I've nothing to do with the cyber attack but that's pretty big bold kind of claim again and creates a little bit of tension between those states which bring us to the second last case study on hype, and in 2015 later the other 15 there was a 10-hour power failure in Turkey.

What I thought was most interesting about this one is in the first couple of hours of that outage occurring before anyone could have possibly had any understanding of root cause analysis or what occurred. We saw significant, primary news sources all around the world from Bloomberg to CNN everywhere saying look because we know that I ran launching cyber attacks against ICS because of the Norse report and because we know that Turkey has been targeted before because of the Bloomberg report on the BTC pipeline. We assess that the turkey pipeline or the turkey blackout might be a cyber attack by Ihram is inappropriate.

In the early hours of outages of any infrastructure going down your state level and national level officials are pretty concerned especially for something like the power grid and for national level leaders to be told by major news outlets that this might be a cyber attack. Mainly when it's built off of previously been debunked excited out stories. You can imagine this increases some level of geopolitical tension at the time in the days following the outage because it takes a while we would find out that the outage was a result of it being one of the hotter days on record. It was overheating the transformers that caused a failure that cascaded across a couple of sites entirely possible utterly reasonable thing to occur. It's just ageing infrastructure. That's why we have to make sure that we're investing in infrastructure and keeping up to date but has nothing to do with cyber. So then the last one that I think is funny unrelated but a good one nevertheless. Conference of bluebells last year where one of the ministers got up and said look it's. This is where we have this conference, and it was the Minister of Energy and Resources in Israel and said Look at this very moment I'm paraphrasing here. Look at this very moment we are experiencing one of the worst cyber attacks in history on our power grid.

That's from a government official if that's decently authoritative, and so CNN and a couple of others ran the headlines. This is a screen capture from one of the news articles Israeli power grid suffers a massive cyber attack that's what was said Unfortunately what the minister meant to say was oh it's in our regulatory authority which has nothing to do with our power grid. Just a small office with like 30 computers and some people. Also, it's what happened has somebody opened up an efficient e-mail that had ransomware on it. So kind of a little bit different than then. Power Grid is suffering massive cyber attack versus in an office completely unrelated to the power grid.

Somebody has ransomware. You got to be a little bit nuanced sometimes. That is, of course, the point as well. We consistently see no matter what happens whether San Francisco and New York both have a small power outage at the same time or whether some train derails.

The first thing people jump to be a cyber attack, and that's not even the most likely scenario. It's possible. We have to be concerned about threats we'll walk through in the second half presentation. However, we got to be a bit more nuanced than this, and a lot of the course they get sometimes captured the media are governor's office not refusing to say that it's not a cyber attack because they have no information. I mean I'm not refusing to say that it wasn't a squirrel but it's not. It's probably not what happened, but I don't know what it wasn't. We don't know what it was. This is honest on this next-gen software we're tech against foreign governments why is our pop up that you need a passive system. I'll get to that later.

Also, my point here is a lot of the stuff that we want to do to be older raise that bar in security and make it where we have very defensible environments. So is the simple stuff I mentioned to begin the presentation that I had been on the offence after my career not penthouse not the red team but somebody else's APT. So I'll note that never in my day did we think to ourselves how am I going to impress the defender when they find me. I think that was that's not the point. The point was you'd got a bunch of missions, and everybody in the world has management PowerPoint. Even your offensive people. Also, so it was this idea of how do we get on with their lives.

How Do We Keep Doing the Mission?
Moreover, there's operational risk in being fancy if you leverage cool tools cool exploits cool tradecraft you're going to call in some senior responders that are going to get raise attention, and it's going to be defensive or softens me very hard on the offence at that point.

However, if I come up with some basic piece of malware on a vulnerability that's existed for five years or something, I'm not losing any tradecraft and not exposing anything that I'm at risk on. Also, more importantly, if you see the adversary at that point well you might bypass something not that important an operational benefit for adversaries being basic and only doing what they need to do to do the mission. So if you're constantly trying to prioritize the next-gen things, but you've missed the Jim things that were supposed to be doing. It might be something to re-evaluate your posture.

Let's talk about real threats and again the problem. So it comes to the ICS community. One of our biggest problems is that there are not many people in this industry the free numbers put there to put it around to be thousand or so ICS cybersecurity professionals worldwide simply not many people. So also we don't know our threat landscape. Also, the chart on the right is metrics from the ICS surge and the fairly authoritative body even though a lot of the metrics are you know it could be a little bit deeper into to realize that there's a problem with a lot of the metrics. However, one of the things that don't get advertised out or catching into the headlines every year is the fact that the number one attack vector every single year into industrial control systems is known the number two attack vector is spearfishing. Except we don't have a lot of e-mail servers and skate environments. So what the metrics are saying is if we see it's because IT catches it going into the ice. Yes but if it's just in the ice. Yes. We have no idea how I got there. Also, many times people have the logging of the visibility set up, so we do need to do better. So we've got to get more visibility into those environments and take a more secure posture because one of the things I love about our industrial infrastructure is it's very defensible. I actually have the position that our ICS infrastructure is more defensible than IT. Especially with the weird systems that we have fiscal engineering the complexity that it takes for an adversary to accomplish a mission that there can be confident that they're going to get the exact output that they're looking for an awesome opportunity and with the right application security we do very well because we do have real threats.

There are plenty of case studies on Insiders causing issues across the industrial community and whether it's at random stories about rail stations or reversing the flow of sewage in Russia Australia. So, of course, there was a big S word right when the Iranian nuclear reactors were physically destroyed centrifuges a Stuxnet Dragonfly back in 2013 the compromised sites around the world and then Dragonfly 2.0 just a little bit earlier this year compromising industrial control system environments and a lot of news coverage to this and oh my gosh they're taking off screenshots of the H.M. eyes with the human-machine interface. We're all going to die. No, we're not we're going to walk through it a couple of minutes on how these attacks occur and the fact that it's a little bit more nuanced than that and an attacker even with direct access controls as an environment is not necessarily going to be able to have a reliable effect. Also, it's not going to be some big cascading failure at that point. We also have electric which was the creators of Crash Override which we'll talk about at the end of this presentation and then Sam worm who is the folks that used it and also took down the green power in 2015 the first cyber attack in history that resulted in outages in a power grid we have seen in Magnolia. There are some groups that we track internally.

Some groups are also targeting industrial sites both in petrochemical and in electric energy. So then, of course, you have tons of this little malware infections, and we've done a ton of resources publicly reference there you can go on YouTube and search for mimics the sands ICF summit and just went out and said Look how many incidental infections occur inside of industrial control environments every year. Let's see if we get some metrics on this and we compile all the data and hunted through it and try to duplicate it and figure that there are around four or five thousand infections per year inside of industrial violence. However, it's things like Conficker and slammer and old malware and often tells people that Conficker has done more damage the American power grid than Iran China and Russia combined. However, we still do to maybe nuance because Conficker is not going to plan out an attack at the right political or the worst time for us. Also, it's not going to be something too complicated whereas a foreign adversary might. So there's a balance that we need to have the highest likelihood is not necessarily the highest risk. So again there are real attacks.

However, let's walk through this if you're going to make an ICS cyber attack. There are some things you're going to have to do it over the sands too. Moreover, I authored a paper years ago titled The ICS cyber filtering and in what we did is we said that there are two stages to an ICS cyber attack. The first stage mimics very closely the cyber kill chain that Lockheed Martin-built years ago. The one that basically all the emphasis community uses to analyze intrusions which is this idea that Navistar is going to do some planning they're going to target environment. Maybe weaponize an e-mail by having malware inside of an attachment send it to somebody they're going to open it up can exploit the system install malware reach back to command control addresses that the adversary owns and then do some traction, and much stuff can happen really quickly.

Minutes or hours or sometimes even just days regarding compromised an entire company after the start of the adversaries campaign and then act phase in a normal IT environment. It might be espionage it might be stealing our life or property. Maybe it's even just ransomware. However, in ICS environments what we're looking for is for the adversary to find access to the operational network and also steal off data related to the industrial network like engineering documents and information about how it's being used. Also, it's not just going to happen in the one company, but it would likely need to happen in a couple of companies especially for more complex systems that depend on each other like electric energy. However, even in petrochemical and manufacturing as an example, they would likely still need to target places like their integrators and figure out the engineering documents and how the system was built and set up because about industrial controls are connected on the network for an IP address.

A lot of its physical engineering process and you got to learn that stuff before you can develop an attack. So once you do all that stage one stuff which is many gatherings of data usually across multiple companies, then you can interpret all that data, and it's not simple to do. You've got to interpret any safety system. Well, the relief wells are there. What's the physical process. How does it how is it the engineering impact the work how does the network impact the engineering?

Is there a way you ultimately will develop knowledge on that industrial environment and with that knowledge you might develop a malicious capability like crash right or you might develop a way that you're going to abuse the ICS against itself.

There doesn't need to be malware involved. It can just be learning to use the industrial equipment against itself. If a skater operator can turn on the lights and turn off the lights using the skater system then so could the adversary.

Then there's also going to need to be some level of testing you're going to have some highly reliable high confidence attack that modifiers and doesn't attack rate modifies the processor destroys equipment or disrupts in some significant way. You're not just going to come out of the lab waste years of resource maybe months of resource months or years of resources millions of dollars and go OK I'm not going to test it, and production is going to push this victim, and we'll see what happens. It's not very likely to occur. Also, then there's me some reading livery.

It is this idea that the adversary has to deliver whatever new knowledge or capability they've developed they're going to either install that malware or modify the access to the system to be able to make their attack. They're ultimately going to execute the attack which could be a variety of different styles of attacks that occur in industrial. We flip back and forth real quick when I say that we have a very proper environment. It's because I'm saying that we have an extended kill chain. Not only do we have complex environments we have extra things that are different than just Windows systems. However, the adversary has to go through more steps. They have to do more things where they can build an environment to mimic, and I mean that we're pretty simply very complex actually to mimic somebody else's entirety of an ICS accurately. It just takes more time which gives defenders an awesome opportunity discover detect and respond to those attackers. We do have real attacks again. So I was one of the lead investigators on the Ukraine attack that happened in 2015, and I've outlined it here. We're not going to go through it in depth.

I want to get to the Crash Override stuff, but I included our report that we published in the right-hand corner. We publish it through Sam's figure the first ever cyber attack on a power grid should likely not be analyzed by vendors, but maybe we should push it out as a sort of a community report as we did. So through Sands, you'll see there that on stage 1 stuff it was all the typical phishing e-mail malware drops. Getting credentials finding an environment that happened in a couple of different energy companies in Ukraine in a matter of days.

When it came down to that stage to stuff where they developed malicious firmware for the even serial devices which brought some sense of

industrial equipment they learned how to operate the distribution management system. Hijack the skating environment away from the operators
to open up the circuit breakers substations that do energize them modifying the backup power on the network to make sure the power dropped
and the control centers malware to delete all the windows systems. The
operators didn't have access to skate at the end telephone analysis service
on the call centre so people couldn't call in when all this stuff that led in
that outage were in those environments for six months before the attack.
I doesn't look like they were waiting around it looks like they were still
learning. Leading up to it much more complicated thing and the crazy
thing is even after the six-month operation they just had six hours of
outage. So it's bad, and it needs to be taken very seriously as a severe red
line was crossed to target civilian infrastructure, but it's still just a six-hour
outage, not the. Build a bunker that we sometimes get exposed to.

Let's look at look at the 2016 one as well. So in 2016 a second attack
by the same group targeting Ukraine again this time targeted different site
instead of 60 additional substations across Ukraine. It just targeted one
little transmission substation but that one transmission a little substation
had three times the power loss of these 60 plus distribution stations across
the country because that's how it works. You have big generation sources
that have a transmission which can lock the back when your country and
then you have the smaller distribution sites for local towns and resto-
ration of power was within 30 to 60 minutes. So only 30 60 an outage.
I think this was probably more testing in my assessment this was the
adversaries were testing their abilities and seeing what they could do more
than having a direct effect of let's have a one-hour outage. However, what
was it and why is it concerning. Well if we look again at that stage 1 Stage
2 thing this attack and everything that we know about it relies on the state
we don't have the instant response data to understand how it got there in
the first place. As far as is where we're you know drag us east were the two
firms that did the analysis on this drag us publish it on the name Crash
Override. Is it published on the name and industry? Also, it was just malware analysis that we're not involved in the investigation or not involved
in the response and that malware analysis that we would do to bring us up
to the community and help inform folks all about what was or what was
being installed and executed.

So it's just the last two. Technically the last four because it was what was what it was what was developed, but we see the installation and execution attack.

Also, that is the malware itself. What was interesting about the malware and I put our paper on it over on the left, there is it had the traditional like here's a back door and a launcher analysts delete some files off the system. What was most interesting about it is it didn't rely on any exploits or vulnerabilities. There was some vulnerability stuff in there that it could leverage, but it had nothing to do with the attack the attack itself was all about learning and codifying industrial operations.

How do I learn how to communicate with electrical equipment to open up circuit breakers to D energized areas. How do I do that and how do I codifying it using the protocols that are used in industrial work like 1 1 1 4 6 1 8 5 0 0 B.C. down the bottom where all ICS network protocols from 0 0 to be protocols they get used.

How can I call that knowledge to let my malware automate this is the exciting thing is in 2015 the attack that occurred when we did have investigation details? It was my assessment to the community that those around 20 people involved in that operation just by the timing of what they were doing it was all manual right there interacting directly with the ICS interacting directly to disconnect the circuit breakers. It's malware that's automated. So really just in one person put it in place and execute it. Also, this isn't something that's going to spread. On top of a ransom where a worm or something. That's not how it works. You've got to put it in place still. So as human operations to limit this from just targeting every site in the world. However, it's still something you can replay and do at other sites. The way that this is built since it's only dependent on electric grid knowledge and not zero days and things like that it would work all across Europe most the Middle East, and most of Asia without any modification. Remember there's still that whole stage one operation that they have a story has to do to get in place. You would need some modification and probably take a day or two of modifying it to get it to work. The United States just based off us being a little bit different in our grid usage but in general this is a pretty scalable piece of malware.

Remember though it's not highly destructive. It's not put it on a piece of work you know put on a worm and spread across the world take it down. It is a one-hour power outage kind of piece of capability, but it is that sweet spot of the difference between scalability and destruction. When you think about it the more complex the system is such as the power grid being very complex, the more complicated it is, the more resources it takes to attack reliably and the larger the impact you want to have. Maybe having days of outages instead of hours. The more resources you have to spend but the more impact you want to have on the more duration you want to have your outage also mean the less scalable it is. So I developed capabilities spread to the entirety of the power grid. I'm going to get a one-hour outage, but if I develop a capability, it's going to destroy equipment and screw a facility like Stuxnet. It's only going to work in Natanz. Now, these are sort of soft rules of thumb we'll see it evolve over the years I'm sure. However, just as a general disparity the more scalable, the more impactful it is and the more sort of more scalable more impactful the more resources that are going to each.

If I want I imagine a sort of invisible knobs here invisible like 1 to 10 meter, I want 10 on the scalability piece it's going to take me an exponential level of resources to do that. I also want it fast rising that disruption and the impact duration piece. It's going to be even harder if it's scalable. So long story short was more scalable less destructive more destructive less scalable, and you can try to increase both, but it takes a ton of resources to do so. So this idea that the grid power lines oil pipeline gasoline all this stuff is going to come down very quickly and it's so easy by the Amazon and all that it just simply misleading.

We have real threats have real concerns. We've got to take it seriously, but we should have a little bit of nuance because a lot of the things that we're looking at even when adversaries get access to an industrial control system and take screenshots it sounds scary. It's like the 20 percent of the effort even getting access this isn't the hard part it's synthesizing all that data and knowing what to do with it to have a reliable, scalable attack on the ICI. I see one of four module crashes all right. The example displayed over and saw ICF that was for you. What happened is a load onto an HDMI communicates to an hour to you which is a type of physical infrastructure that's controlling circuit breakers. Just open the circuit breaker so really the entire attack was sending legitimate commands to open up the circuit breaker system vulnerabilities. Again there's something about the protocols that need to change encrypting it wouldn't have done anything.

The protocols don't have vulnerabilities it's just that's how the electric grid works. So once the attacker gets in and learns how to do that, then it's not too complicated for them to repeat that. However, again that nuances takes a while to get there. Takes much effort and even at the high end, we've only seen a couple of hours of outages. So we end the presentation and take questions for like five or six minutes we have left want to leave you with something. Since we've, we've talked about there being much hype we're got to have nuance. We've talked about threats that are real and serious. One of the papers I wrote a couple of years ago was called the sliding scale of cybersecurity and position the five categories of things you can do to increase security. So as you go back out into the world and you try to do security thinking about these five categories and know that the most return on investment the most significant value is on the left-hand side of the scale. Building something right from the first time putting logging in place security in the design of a good software development engineering.

All of this is the sweet spot when we identify weaknesses we'll put things like passive defences on the same security technologies and tools and firewalls and intrusion detection systems. Defence is people getting involved. The human component of security instant response threat hunting that we're pretty monitoring intelligence is that collecting and analyzing adversary information to create intelligence helps us prioritize and address knowledge gaps in the organization and the offence. I have on there is technically you could do office to increase security but seeing how I see a lot of this discussion these days, I want to note all this hack back kind of stuff. One of the real reasons I built this scale was to show that regardless of your ethical views of it it's just not a good return on investment in resources and I have to bluntly tell folks sometimes if you suck at Defense you're going to suck it offence. So we have many opportunities to do real defence. We don't need to get scared. We don't need to have fear driver decisions. We don't need to let things excite us out, and we don't need to be thinking about going back after the adversaries.

We have all the tools that we need to be successful. So with that I'll go and take the questions over on the side I'll repeat them back to you. Also, of course afterwards always feel free to get in touch with me. I'll know that the easiest way is I'm on Twitter quite a bit more responsible than e-mails. However, the first question what do you suggest will help most with research and this little bit vague form of research into what areas if you have time to sort of back in the chat.

However, I'll note that in general when I look into research and ICS security, I often find that people are taking IT security best practices and copy and paste them into ICS and it can be dangerous. It's not just necessarily a bad practice. It can be dangerous in environments that we're dealing with human life and the safety of the people and the environment. I'd prefer to see instead as people understand what our risks are and learn from the threat landscape learned from what they are doing and understanding how we're going to take unique tradecraft and capabilities. Codify best practices and make sure that our security practices are paired with a real understanding of the risk we're trying to reduce. So with research, it's many times not about the systems themselves.

I see many folks want to research finding vulnerabilities on controlling the vulnerabilities in control it might not even be the point. Sometimes they're not. ICS own abilities no a significant majority of them I think a couple of people publicly done the research and stated around 90 something per cent of them are just trash they're they don't introduce new risk. They're just some hacking kind of stuff. Moreover, what I want to enforce by that is remember it's about the physics about the engineering it's about the process. It's about the people the research into this should be able to figure out how to complement the mission not restricted and how do we make sure that we're addressing the real threats to reduce real risk instead of addressing with resources the hype that one's which ultimately aren't helping us out. Good question. So how do you think the media should behave in these situations. I have seen many journalists get much better at this over years of working with a couple of them and they're getting pretty good. We're getting journalists that will get a vendor pitch, or they'll get a government official wanting to leak something, or they'll hear about one of these big cyber attacks, and they reach out to subject matter experts instead of finding somebody who understands industrial control systems. Ask a couple of people because sometimes there might be differences in opinions and figure out what that risk is. Also, if it's significant then feel free to report on it. However, if it's efficient e-mail a couple of energy companies. That's not a big deal. So my significant problem here is I'm not concerned about the grid failing. I think that it's the very unlikely scenario not even unlikely. It's just it is there's much complexity in that topic. Probably for another day. However, I'm worried about maybe an adversary taking down Washington D.C. or San Francisco for three hours you know politically that that changes things. When the American public is fearful or when that's the psychology of things changes you know that's an issue. Alternatively, maybe even an accidental attack. One attacker didn't mean to take something down it does. How do we deal with that where it looks like an act of war. It's not. I'm concerned about the fear driving policy decisions. I'm concerned about our fear I'm hindering good policy decisions. So sometimes that media hype weighs very heavily with politicians regulations and influences things worse than an attack ever could. Also, then the last question in the last 30 seconds if the attackers can generalize this attack in the future do you think these attacks me done by script kiddies. I don't think so. So even when we see Crash Override which was that again that sweet spot of scalability with some level of outages it still required all those stage one operations to target a company do the operations get it in place and then actually execute the attack that requires resources. It's merely not trivial. We are still ways off and we still need to do a lot of work to secure our infrastructures."

Index of Key Terms

Backdoor

Entering a protected system utilizing a password could be described as going through the front door. Businesses may build "backdoors" in their programs, however, so that developers can bypass authentication and dive directly into the app. Backdoors are often secret but might be manipulated by hackers if they're revealed or discovered.

Black-Hat

A person who hacks for private gain or who participates in illegal and unsanctioned activities. Rather than white hack hackers, who hack to be able to alert businesses and enhance black hat hackers can instead sell the flaws, they discover to other hackers or utilize them.

Botnet

Botnets are networks of computers controlled by an attacker. Having control over hundreds of computers allows terrible actors to perform particular types of cyber attacks, including a DDoS (see the following). Buying thousands of computers would not be economical, however, so hackers deploy malware to infect arbitrary computers which are connected to the web.

Brute Force

A brute force attack will often consist of an automated procedure of trial-and-error to figure the correct passphrase. Most modern encryption methods use different procedures for slowing down brute force attacks, which makes it difficult or impossible to test all combinations in a reasonable period.

Cracking

A general term to describe entering into a security system without authorization. Hackers are tinkerers; they are not necessarily evil men. Crackers are malicious.

Crypto

Brief for cryptography, the science of secret communication or the procedures and procedures for hiding messages and data with encryption (see the following).

Chip-Off

A chip-off assault requires the user to remove memory storage chips in a device so that information could be scraped from them using specialized applications. This attack was used by law enforcement to break into PGP-protected Blackberry phones.

Dark Web

The dark web is composed of sites that aren't indexed by Google and are only available through specialization networks like Tor (see the following). Frequently, the darknet is used by site operators that wish to remain anonymous. Everything on the darknet is on the deep web, but not everything on the deep web is on the darknet.

DDoS

DDoS is Distributed Denial of Service Attack. This results in the goal, to slow down a website or make it inaccessible. Attackers can also use the easier Denial of Service attack, which can be launched from one computer.

Deep Web

This term and "dark web" or "dark web" are sometimes used interchangeably, even though they should not be. The deep web is the region of the Internet that's not indexed by search engines.

Digital Certificate

An electronic passport or stamp of approval that demonstrates the identity of an individual, website or service online. In more technical terms, a digital certification demonstrates that someone is in possession of a particular cryptographic key that, traditionally, cannot be forged. Some of the most popular digital certificates are those of sites, which guarantee your link to them is appropriately encrypted. These get displayed in your browser as a green padlock.

Encryption

The process of scrambling messages or data was making it unreadable and confidential. The reverse is decryption, the decoding of the message. Both encryption and decryption are acts of cryptography. Encryption is used by individuals and corporations and in electronic security for customer products.

End-to-End Encryption

A specific sort of encryption in which a message or data gets scrambled or encoded on one end, such as your pc or telephone, and receive decrypted on the other end, like somebody else's computer.

Evil Maid Assault

As the name probably suggests an evil maid assault is a hack which needs physical access to a computer—the sort of access a wicked maid may have while tidying her or his employer's office, for instance.

Exploit

An exploit is a method or process to take advantage of a bug or vulnerability in a computer or program. Not all bugs cause exploits. Consider it this way: If your door was faulty, it might be just that it makes a weird sound when you start it, or that its lock can be chosen. Both are defects, but only one can assist a burglar to get in. The way the offender picks the lock is the exploit.

Forensics

On CSI, forensic investigations involve a set of exact steps to be able to establish what occurred during a crime. In regards to a hack, however, investigators are searching for digital fingerprints rather than physical ones. This procedure usually involves trying to retrieve messages or other information from a device—may be a phone, a desktop computer or a server—used, or abused, by a suspected offender.

GCHQ

The UK's equivalent of the NSA. "As these adversaries operate secretly, so too must GCHQ," the company says on its site. "We can't disclose publicly everything that we do, but we remain fully accountable."

Hacker

This term is now—wrongly—interchangeable with somebody who breaks into systems or hacks things digitally. Initially, hackers were just tinkerers or individuals who appreciated "exploring the details of programmable systems and how to stretch their capabilities."

Hacktivist

A "hacktivist" is somebody who uses their hacking abilities for political ends. A hacktivist's actions could be small, like defacing the public site of a safety service or other government department, or large, like concealing sensitive government information and distributing it to taxpayers. 1 often-cited illustration of a hacktivist group is Anonymous.

Hashing

Say you have a bit of text which should stay confidential, like a password. You can store the text in a secret folder on your device, but if anybody gained access to it, you would be in trouble. To maintain the password a secret, you could also "hash" it using a program that implements a function leading to garbled text representing the original details. This abstract representation is called a hash.

HTTPS/SSL/TLS

Stands for Hypertext Transfer Protocol, with the "S" for "Secure." HTTPS uses the protocols SSL and TLS to not only shield your relationship but also to show the identity of the website, so that if you type https://gmail.com, you can be confident you are connecting to Google rather than an imposter website.

Infosec

An abbreviation of "Information Security." It is the inside baseball term for what is more commonly called cybersecurity, a term that irks most people who favor infosec.

Jailbreak

Circumventing the safety of a device, such as an iPhone or a PlayStation, to eliminate a manufacturer's restrictions, generally with the aim to make it run applications from non-official sources.

Keys

Modern cryptography uses digital "keys." In other systems, there might only be one key that is shared with all parties. Either way, if an attacker gains control of the key which does the unlocking, they might have a fantastic chance at gaining entry to.

Lulz

An Internet-speak variant on "lol" (short for "laughing out loud") employed regularly among the black hat hacker set, typically to warrant a hack or flow done at the cost of another individual or entity.

Malware

Stands for "malicious software." It merely refers to any malicious program or software, designed to hack or damage its target.

Man-in-the-Middle

A Man-in-the-Middle or MitM is a frequent attack where someone surreptitiously places themselves between two parties, impersonating them. This permits the malicious attacker to intercept and possibly alter their communication. With this sort of attack, an individual can passively listen to, relaying messages and information between the two parties, or even change and manipulate the data stream.

Metadata

Metadata is just data about data. In the event you should send an e-mail, by way of example, the text you type for your buddy is going to be the content of this message.

NIST

The National Institute of Standards and Technology is an extension of the US Department of Commerce committed to science and metrics that support industrial innovation.

Nonce

A portmanteau of the amount and after, nonce means "a number only used once." It is a series of numbers generated by a system to identify an individual to get a one-time-use session or particular job. Following that session, or a predetermined period, the number is not used again.

OpSec

OpSec is short for operational safety, and it is all about keeping information confidential, off and online. "Great" OpSec will flow out there and might include everything from passing messages on Post-Its rather than e-mails to using digital encryption. Quite simply: Loose tweets destroy fleets.

OTR

What should you do if you wish an encrypted conversation, but it needs to happen quickly? OTR is a protocol for encrypting instant messages end-to-end. Unlike PGP, OTR employs a single temporary key for each conversation.

Password Managers

Employing the same, crummy password for all your logins—from the bank accounts to Seamless, to your Tinder profile—is a bad idea. Memorizing a unique string of characters for each platform is daunting. All you want to remember is your master password to log into the manager and get all your many different logins.

Penetration testing or Pentesting

If you establish a security system for your home, or your office, or your factory, you would want to make sure it was protected from attackers, right? 1 way to check a system's security would be to employ individuals—pentesters—to hack it to spot weak points purposely. Pentesting is associated with red teaming, even though it could be performed in a more organized, less competitive manner.

PGP

"Pretty Good Privacy" is a way of encrypting data, normally mails, so that anyone intercepting them will only see garbled text. PGP uses asymmetric cryptography, meaning the individual sending a message uses a "people" encryption key to scramble it, and the receiver uses a key "private" key to decode it. Despite being more than two years old, PGP is still a powerful technique of encryption, though it can be notoriously hard to use in practice, even for seasoned users.

Phishing

Phishing is more of a kind of social engineering than hacking or cracking. In a phishing process, an attacker typically reaches out to a victim to extract specific information which can be utilized in a subsequent attack. That may indicate posing as consumer service from Google, Facebook, or the victim's cell phone provider, by way of instance, and asking the victim to click on a malicious link—or just asking the victim to send back information, like a password, in an e-mail. Attackers usually burst out phishing efforts by the thousands, but occasionally employ more concentrated attacks, called spearphishing (see the following).

Plaintext

What it sounds like—text which hasn't been garbled with encryption. This definition could be considered plaintext. You could also hear plaintext being known as "cleartext," because it refers to text that's being kept out in the open, or "in the clear."

Pwned

Pwned is computer nerd jargon (or "leetspeak") for the verb "own." In the video game world, a player that beat another player can say he pwned him. Among hackers, the expression has a similar meaning, rather than beating someone in a match, a hacker who has gained access to another user's computer can say he pwned him.

RAT

RAT stands for Remote Access Tool or Remote Access Trojan. RATs are scary when used as malware. An attacker who successfully installs a RAT in your computer can gain complete control of your system. There's also a legitimate business in RATs for men and women that wish to access their office computer from home, and so on. The worst part about RATs? Many malicious ones can be found in the net's underground available or even at no cost, so attackers can be entirely unskilled and use this sophisticated tool.

Ransomware

Ransomware is a sort of malware that protects your personal computer and will not allow you to access your files. You will see a message that informs you just how much the ransom is and where to send payment, usually requested in bitcoin, to get your files back. This is a fantastic racket for hackers, and that's why many believe it currently an "outbreak," as individuals typically are prepared to pay a couple of hundred bucks to recoup their machine. It's not only individuals, either. In ancient 2016, the Hollywood Presbyterian Medical Center in Los Angeles paid approximately $17,000 after being struck by a ransomware assault.

Rainbow Table

A rainbow table is a sophisticated technique which enables hackers to simplify the process of imagining what passwords are behind a "hash" (as shown earlier).

Red Team

To guarantee the safety of the computer systems and to suss out any unknown vulnerabilities, businesses can hire hackers who arrange into a "red team" to be able to run oppositional strikes against the system and try to take it over completely. In these instances, being hacked is a fantastic thing because organizations can fix vulnerabilities before somebody who is not on their citizenship does. Red teaming is a general concept that's employed across several sectors, including military plan.

Root

In most computers, "origin" is the usual name given to the most basic (and thus most powerful) degree of accessibility in the machine, or is the name for the account which has those privileges. That means the "origin" can install software, delete and create files. If a hacker "earnings root," they can do anything they want on the system or computer they compromised. This is the holy grail of hacking.

Rootkit

A rootkit is a specific kind of malware which resides deep in your system and is triggered whenever you boot it up, even before your operating system begins. This makes rootkits challenging to detect, persistent and can capture practically all information on the infected computer.

Salting

When protecting text or passwords, "hashing" (as shown earlier) is a basic process which turns the plaintext into garbled text. To create hashing even more successful, individuals or companies can add a collection of random bytes, called a "salt," into the password before the hashing procedure. This adds the layer of protection.

Script Kiddies

This is a derisive term for somebody that has a small bit of computer savvy and who is only able to utilize off-the-shelf applications to do things like knock sites offline or sniff passwords within an unprotected Wi-Fi access point. This is necessarily a term to discredit somebody who claims to be a proficient hacker.

Shodan

It has been known as "hacker's Google," and a "terrifying" search engine. Consider it as a Google, but for connected devices as opposed to websites. Utilizing Shodan is possible to discover unprotected webcams, baby monitors, printers, medical apparatus, gasoline pumps, and even wind turbines. While that sounds frightening, Shodan's value is precisely what it helps researchers locate these devices and alert their owners so that they can secure them.

Signature

Another purpose of PGP is your ability to "sign" messages along with your key encryption key. Because this key is only known to an individual and is stored on their computer and nowhere else, cryptographic signatures should confirm that the person whom you believe you are talking to is that individual. This is a fantastic way to show that you are whom you claim to be on the net.

Side Channel Attack

Your computer's hardware is always emitting a continuous flow of barely-perceptible electrical signals. A side-channel attack attempts to identify patterns in these signs to be able to learn what sort of computations the machine is performing. By way of instance, a hacker "listening in" to a hard drive whirring away while creating a secret encryption key may have the ability to reconstruct that key, effectively stealing it, without your knowledge.

Sniffing

Sniffing is a means of intercepting data sent over a network without being detected, using specific sniffer program. Once the information is gathered, a hacker can sift through it to find useful information, like passwords. It is regarded as a particularly dangerous hack as it's tough to detect and can be done from within or outside a network.

Social Engineering

Not all hacks are performed by staring at a Matrix-like display of green text. From time to time, gaining entrance to a protected system is as simple as placing a telephone call or sending an e-mail and pretending to be someone else—specifically, someone who frequently has access to the said system but forgot their password daily. Phishing (as mentioned earlier) strikes include aspects of social engineering since they involve convincing a person of an e-mail sender's legitimacy before anything else.

Spear-Phishing

Phishing and spearphishing are frequently used interchangeably, but the latter is a more simple, targeted form of phishing (shown earlier), where hackers attempt to trick victims into clicking malicious attachments or links pretending to be proximity, as opposed to a more generic sender, as a social network or company. When done well, spearphishing can be particularly useful and powerful.

Spoofing

Hackers can deceive people into falling for a phishing attack (mentioned earlier) by minding their e-mail address, as an example, which makes it look like the speech of someone the target understands. That's spoofing. It can also be utilized in telephone scams, or to make a fake site address.

Spyware

A particular type of malware of malicious software designed to spy, track, and steal information from the target.

State Actor

State actors are hackers or groups of hackers that are backed by a government, which might be the US, Russia, or China. These hackers are frequently the most powerful since they possess nearly unlimited legal and fiscal resources of a nation-state to back them up. Think, for example, of the NSA. At times, however, state actors may also be a group of hackers that get tacit (or at least hidden from the public) support from their governments, like the Syrian Electronic Army.

Threat Model

Imagine a game of chess. It is your turn, and you are thinking about all of the potential moves your opponent could make, as many turns ahead as possible. Have you left your queen unprotected? Is your king being worked into a corner checkmate? That sort of thinking is precisely what security researchers do when designing a threat model. It is a catch-all term used to describe the capabilities of the enemy that you need to guard against, and your vulnerabilities. Are you an activist trying to shield against a state-sponsored hacking group? Your hazard model better is quite robust. Just shoring up the network in your log cabin in the middle of nowhere? Perhaps not as much cause to worry.

Token

A tiny physical device which enables its owner to log in or authenticate into a service. Tokens serve as an additional layer of security in addition to a password, for instance. The point is that even when the password or key gets stolen, the hacker would want the real physical token to misuse it.

Tor

Tor is short for The Onion Router. Initially developed by the United States Naval Research Laboratory, it is now used by bad guys (hackers, cyber-criminals) and activists or journalists to anonymize their actions online. The basic idea is that there's a network of computers around the world—some operated by universities, some by people, some by the government—which will route your visitors in byzantine ways to be able to conceal your actual location. The Tor system is this assortment of volunteer-run computers. The Tor Project is the nonprofit that maintains the Tor software. The Tor browser is the utterly free bit of software which lets you use Tor. Tor hidden services are sites which can only be obtained through Tor.

Tails

Tails stand for The Amnesic Incognito Live System. If you are serious about electronic security, this is the operating system supported by

Edward Snowden. Tails is an amnesic system so that your computer remembers nothing; it is like a new machine each time you boot up. The program is a free and open source. While it's well-regarded, safety defects have been discovered.

Verification (Ditch)

The procedure by which reporters and safety researchers undergo hacked data and be sure it's legitimate. This practice is essential to be sure that the information is authentic, and the claims of anonymous hackers are accurate, rather than merely an effort to get some notoriety or make some money scamming people on the darknet.

VPN

VPN stands for Virtual Private Network. VPNs use encryption to make a personal and secure channel to connect to the net when you are on a network you do not trust (say a Starbucks or an Airbnb WiFi). Consider a VPN as a tube from you to your destination, dug beneath the standard Internet. VPNs make it possible for employees to connect to their company's network remotely, and help regular individuals protect their connection. VPNs also allow users to bounce off servers from different areas of the world, permitting them to look as though they're linking from there. This gives them the opportunity to bypass censorship, such as China's Great Firewall, or see Netflix's US offerings while in Canada. There are unlimited VPNs, which makes it almost impossible to choose which ones are the best.

Virus

A computer virus is a type of malware that typically is embedded and hidden in a file or program. Unlike a worm (see the following), it requires human action to disperse (for example, an individual forwarding a virus-infected attachment, or downloading a malicious software) Viruses can infect computers and steal data, delete data, encrypt it or mess with it in practically any other way.

Vuln

Abbreviation for "vulnerability." Another way to refer to bugs or software defects which may be exploited by hackers.

Warez

Pronounced like the contraction for "where is," warez describes pirated software that is typically distributed via technologies such as BitTorrent and Usenet. Warez is sometimes laden with malware, taking advantage of people's desire for free software.

White Hat

A white hat hacker is a person who hacks with the objective of fixing and shielding systems. Rather than black hat hackers (shown earlier), rather than taking advantage of the hacks or the bugs they find to create money illegally, they alert the firms and even help them fix the problem.

Worm

A particular type of malware that propagates and reproduces itself, spreading from computer to computer. The net's history is littered with worms, from the Morris worm, the first of its type, and the renowned Samy worm, which infected more than a million people on MySpace.

Zero-Day

A zero-day or "0 day" is a bug that is unknown to the software vendor, or at least it is not patched yet. The title stems from the notion that there have been zero days involving the discovery of this bug or flaw and the first attack using it. Zero-days would be the most prized bugs and exploits for hackers since a fix has not yet been set up for them, so they are almost certain to work.

References

"10 Disturbing And Crazy Facts About the Deep Web You" http://canyouactually. com/10-disturbing-and-crazy-facts-about-the-deep-web-you-probably-never-knew/

Alperovitch, D. 2016. "Bears in the Midst: Intrusion into the Democratic National Committee." *Crowdstrike Blog.* June 15, available from www.crowdstrike. com/blog/bears-midst-intrusion-democratic-national-committee/

Amato, J. 1996. "LA Times Story on AOL Phishers, Alt.Aol-Sucks Newsgroup." May 13, available from https://groups.google.com/forum/m/#!search/ phishing$20aohell$20alt.aol-sucks/alt.aol-sucks/dc5ll928b2U

Assange, J. 2016. "The Podesta E-mails; Part One." *Wikileaks.* October 7, available from: https://wikileaks.org/podesta-emails/press-release

Assange on Peston on Sunday: "More Clinton Leaks to Come." 2016. *ITV News.* June 12, available from www.itv.com/news/update/2016–06-12/assange-on-peston-on-sunday-more-clinton-leaks-to-come

Attackers Deploy New ICS Attack Framework "TRITON" https:// securityboulevard.com/2017/12/attackers-deploy-new-ics-attack-framework-triton-and-cause-operationaldisruption-to-critical-infrastructure/

Barton. 1996. "How AOL Could Stop Account Phishing Tomorrow, Alt.Aol-Sucks Newsgroup." February 5, available from https://groups.google.com/d/ topic/alt.aol-sucks/eNjlyDPjtEo/discussion

Bilton, N. 2016. "How the Clinton Campaign is Foiling the Kremlin." *Vanity Fair.* August 26, available from www.vanityfair.com/news/2016/08/how-the-clinton-campaign-is-foiling-the-kremlin

Brinkbäumer, K., and B. Sandberg. 2017. "It is Soul-Crushing! Clinton Campaign Chair John Podesta on President Trump." *Der Spiegel.* May 5, available from: www.spiegel.de/international/world/clinton-campaign-chair-john-podesta-on-president-trump-a-1146317.html

Borchers, C. 2016. "Reported E-mail Hack Purports to Show Clinton Campaign Tracking Snoopy Reporters." *The Washington Post.* June 28, available from www.washingtonpost.com/news/the-fix/wp/2016/06/28/reported-email-hack-purports-to-show-clinton-campaign-tracking-snoopy-reporters/

Clinton, H. 2017. *What Happened.* New York, NY: Simon and Schuster.

DHS Press Office . 2016. "Joint Statement from the Department of Homeland Security and Officer of the Director of National Intelligence on Election Security." *US Department of Homeland Security.* October 7, available from www.dhs.gov/news/2016/10/07/joint-statement-department-homeland-security-and-office-director-national

Executive summary of Grizzly Steppe findings from Homeland Security Assistant Secretary for Public Affairs Todd Breasseale. 2016. "US Department of Homeland Security." December 30, Available from: www.dhs.gov/news/2016/12/30/executive-summary-grizzly-steppe-findings-homeland-security-assistant-secretary

Franceschi-Bicchierai, L. 2016. "'Guccifer 2.0' is Likely a Russian Government Attempt to Cover Up Its Own Hack." *Motherboard*. June 16, available from https://motherboard.vice.com/en_us/article/wnxgwq/guccifer-20-is-likely-a-russian-government-attempt-to-cover-up-their-own-hack

Gott, A. 2016. "New Study: The One Big Security Trick People Aren't Using, LastPass blog." August 2, available from https://blog.lastpass.com/2016/08/new-study-the-one-big-security-trick-people-arent-using.html/

Guccifer 2.0. 2016. "Guccifer 2.0 DNC's Servers Hacked by a Lone Hacker." *Guccifer 2.0 Blog*, June 15, available from https://guccifer2.wordpress.com/2016/06/15/dnc/

"'Industroyer' ICS Malware Linked to Ukraine Power Grid." 2017. https://securityweek.com/industroyer-ics-malware-linked-ukraine-power-grid-attack

Langberg, M. 1995. "AOL Acts to Thwart Hackers, SF Mercury News." September 8, available from https://simson.net/clips/1995/95.SJMN.AOL_Hackers.html

Leopold, J. 2017. "He Solved the DNC Hack. Now He's Telling his Story for the First Time." *Buzzfeed.com*. November, 8, available from www.buzzfeed.com/jasonleopold/he-solved-the-dnc-hack-now-hes-telling-his-story-for-the

Lipton, E., D. Sanger., and S. Shane. 2016. "The Perfect Weapon: How Russian Cyber Power Invaded the U.S., New York Times." December 13, available from www.nytimes.com/2016/12/13/us/politics/russia-hack-election-dnc.html?mtrref=t.co&_r=0

"Meet Your Army: Warrant Officer Heads up Army's Maritime." https://army.mil/article/177084/meet_your_army_warrant_officer_heads_up_armys_maritime_training

Multi Factor Authentication—Office 365|Information https://fairmontstate.edu/it/multi-factor-authentication-office-365

Nakashima, R., and B. Ortutay. 2017. "AP Exclusive: Russia Twitter Trolls Deflected Trump Bad News." Associated Press. November 10, available from https://apnews.com/fc9ab2b0bbc34f11bc10714100318ae1

NiGHTS into Dreams.com. http://nightsintodreams.com/

Satter, R. 2017. "Inside Story: How Russians Hacked the Democrats' E-mails." *Associated Press*. November 4, available from https://apnews.com/dea73efc01594839957c3c9a6c962b8a 10 Threat Group-4127 targets Hillary Clinton presidential campaign, Secureworks Counter Threat Unit Threat Intelligence, June 16, 2016, available from https://secureworks.com/research/threat-group-4127-targets-hillary-clinton-presidential-campaign

"Stuxnet Patient Zero: First Victims of the Infamous Worm." 2014. https://
    drasticnews.com/stuxnet-patient-zero-first-victims-of-the-infamous-worm-
    revealed/

Tait, M (as @PwnAllTheThings on Twitter). 2017. "The Takeaway is this: your
    Personal E-mail is the Portal to Everything you do Online." *If It Is Compromised
    All of Your Other Accounts Fall, Twitter.com*, August 16, available from
    https://twitter.com/pwnallthethings/status/897932050111406081

The Rise of ICS Malware: How Industrial Security Threats. 2018. https://
    securityweek.com/rise-ics-malware-how-industrial-security-threats-are-
    becoming-more-surgical

The Motherboard e-Glossary of Cyber Terms and Hacking. 2016. https://
    motherboard.vice.com/en_us/article/mg79v4/hacking-glossary

Thomas, K., F. Li, A. Zand, J. Barrett, J. Ranieri, L. Invernizzi, and D.
    Margolis. 2017. "Data Breaches, Phishing or Malware? Understanding
    the Risks of Stolen Credentials." *Google.Com*, October 30, available from
    https://static.googleusercontent.com/media/research.google.com/en//pubs/
    archive/46437.pdf

Trump, D. 2016. "Very Little Pick-up by the Dishonest Media of Incredible
    Information Provided by WikiLeaks." *So Dishonest! Rigged System!, Twitter.
    com*. October 12, available from https://twitter.com/realDonaldTrump/

"Trump Pulling Out of Iran Deal—TheStreet." 2018. https://thestreet.com/
    politics/trump-reportedly-pulling-out-of-iran-deal-14583314

(unsigned). 2016. "DNC Hacker Releases Trump Oppo Report." *The Smoking
    Gun*. June 15, available from www.thesmokinggun.com/documents/crime/
    dnc-hacker-leaks-trump-oppo-report-647293

(unsigned). 2016. "Hack Yields Clinton Campaign E-mail, Records." *The Smoking
    Gun*. June 28, available from http://thesmokinggun.com/documents/crime/
    hfa-gmail-attack-723571 18

"Webinar—Pulse Surveys|What, When, How and Why?|Qualtrics." https://
    qualtrics.com/events/pulse-surveys-what-when-how-why/

"White Paper: The Deep Web: Surfacing Hidden Value." http://brightplanet.
    com/wp-content/uploads/2012/03/12550176481-deepwebwhitepaper1.pdf

About the Author

Giulio D'Agostino is a system administrator, author, and technologist with more than 20 years of experience in the cloud computing, software as a service, and publishing. Previously worked for Google, Apple, Hewlett Packard, and Salesforce.com. Giulio has lectured at the Technical University of Denmark–DTU, Web Summit 2016/2017 and is currently the system administrator for the software as a service and cloud-based provider company LogMeIn Inc.

Index

A1d3n
  AES, 105, 106
  BTC address, 105
  CloudFlare, 111
  creepypastas, 114
  deep web hosting, 107–109
  DW chats/IRCs, 105–107, 111
  gpg warning, 113–114
  hacktivists/activists encounter,
      111–113
  KIST algorithm, 113, 114
  mobile devices, 115–117
  non-JS webchats, 115
  OMEMO plugin, 107
  onion directories, 110
  ooniprobe project, 114
  Penetration Testing Linux
      distributions, 110
  PHP-based chats, 107, 111, 115
  privacy hacktivist, 104
  Qubes, 110
  terms and conditions update,
      technology companies,
      108–109
  3DES, 105, 106
  Tor/I2P, 109
  VPN, 113
  VPS, 109
Advanced Encryption Standard
    (AES), 97, 100
Advanced Network Research Group
    (ANRG), 21
Advanced persistent threat (APT),
    1, 21
AES. See Advanced Encryption
    Standard (AES)
Ahmia.fi, 108
Ahmia search system, 3
AI, 83
Anonymous, 79
Anonymous online, 36–39

ANRG. See Advanced Network
    Research Group (ANRG)
AOL Instant Messenger, 88
AOL policy, 88
APT. See Advanced persistent threat
    (APT)
APT28, 94
ASTM Ellan javascript HP, 34
Asymmetric cryptography, 98
Asymmetric encryption, 98–99
Atlayo, 84–85
  A1d3n, 104–117
  Mr. Security, 84–96

Backdoor, 57, 58, 120
BAE Systems, 7
Behavior patterns, 39
Big data methods, 22–23
Biometrics, 38
Bitcoin-based drug dealing site, 59
BlackArch, 110
Black-hat, 64, 74, 84
Blowfish, 98
Botnet, 9, 19, 24
Brave browser, 109
Brute force, 102,
BTC pipeline, Turkey, 126–127

Caesar cypher, 101, 102
Canvas tools, 16
Chinese cyber espionage, 27
Chip-off, 139
Cicada 3301, Th Stg
  Anonymous and Wikileaks, 79
  Book of Enoch by John Dee, 80
  Da Vinci code, decipher key, 84
  Dawkins fascination, 81
  enlightenment, 80
  ESP and SSP perception, 80
  human ego, 81
  "human hybrid" access, 80

imagination and pilgrimage, 79
language, 79, 83
morphogenetic fields, Sheldrake
    concept of, 81
open education messages, 81
PGP encrypted messages, 82
privacy, definitions of, 78
self-reliance and privacy
    preservation, 77–78
Simulacra and Simulation by Jean
    Baudril, 80
Sumerian myth, 80
technological renaissance, 76,
    82–83
technology with imagination, 82
work of Bruno Borges, 79–80
C2 infrastructure, 25
Citadel, 8–9
Clearnet, 1
CloudFlare, 111
Club Hell, 96–97
Colonel Gardner, 124, 126
Commodity threats, 25
Comparison interrupted time series
    (C/ITS) analysis, 23
Conficker, 130
Cozy Bear, 94
Cracking, 37, 90, 100
Crossover cable, 74
Crowdstrike, 94
Cryptanalysis, 102
Crypto
    containers, 9
    jacking, 25
Cryptography, 104
    asymmetric, 98
    primer, 96
    symmetric, 97
    wireless, 100–101
A Cryptography primer, 96–97
Cybersecurity
    of civil society organizations, 23
    CrowdStrike, 118
    digital hygiene, 26
    epidemiology paradigm, 24
    market, 63
    NGOs, 26
    public health interventions, 23–24
    sliding scale, 136

VPN, 42
Cyber Security Assessment and
    Response (CyberSAR) project,
    20–21
participants, 26

Dark Internet, 2
Dark net
    ARPA, 57
    vs. dark web, 55
    vs. deep web, 31–36
    for good, 57–58
    infiltrate, 58–59
    intelligence, 58–59
Dark web, 2
    Ahmia, 3
    vs. dark net, 55
    Free Search Methods, 6
    GitHub and SourceForge, 13
    Grams, 4
    hacking tools, 7
    Hidden Wiki, 2–3
    hybrid methods, 8
    KelvinSecTeam, definition by,
        54–55
    mobile applications, 8
    multiple exploits method, 8
    Not Evil, 4–5
    Onion Link, 5
    SQL injection, 11
    Surface Web and Dark Internet
        websites, 2, 7
    threat intelligence, 55–56
        actuarial mathematical science,
            63–64
        Amber Alerts, 63
        catch rate, 61
        degree of rigor, 63
        immediate value and security
            growth, 59–60
        insurance companies, 63
        intelligence programs, 61–62
        intrusion prevention services,
            61
        mathematical sophistication,
            63
        meta information, 62
        return on investment, 61
        risk scoring, 63

scans and trends, 62
vulnerabilities and attack
    information, 62
Torch, 5
traffic tracking, 59
user's information, 7
DarpaMemex directory page, 13
DARPA's Memex search tool, 110
Darpa software, 13–17
Data compression, 65
Da Vinci code, decipher key, 84
DaVinci tools, 15
Dawkins fascination, 81
DDoS. *See* Denial-of-service attacks
    (DDoS)
Debian Linux, 77
DeepPeep, 108
DeepSound, 67
Deep web, 1
    anonymous online, 36–39
    Citadel, 8–9
    vs. dark net, 31–36
    ElcomSoft, 9–10
    EnCase, 10
    hacking tools, 6–7
    hybrid methods, 8
    Joseph definition, 27
    Kali Linux, 10–11
    Maltego, 11
    malware, 6, 7
    Metasploit, 11–12
    Nmap, 12–13
    "spoofing" technique, 7
Deep Web Technologies, 108
Denial-of-service attacks (DDoS), 119
DES, 97
Dictionary attack, encrypted
    passwords, 89
Diffie-Hellman, 98
Digital certificate, 140
Digital hygiene, 26
Digital Insecurity in Context, 22
Digital security environment, 25
Digital steganography, 64, 65
Digital threats, 25
DNC, 93–96
DNS. *See* Domain Name Service
    (DNS)
Documented attacks, 25

Domain Name Service (DNS)
    firewall, 25
    leaking, 52–53
    traffic, 24
Dossier Stack, 13
Dot onion sites, 48, 50
Dragonfly 2.0, 130
DuckDuckGo, 112

ECC. *See* Elliptical curve
    cryptography (ECC)
EFNet, 13
ElcomSoft, 9–10
Elliptical curve cryptography (ECC),
    99
e-mail, Mr. Security, 84–96
EnCase, 10
Encryption, 7, 39, 52, 103, 104
    AES, 106
    algorithms, 101, 102
    asymmetric, 98–99
    Citadel, 9
    communication, 112
    data, 41, 65
    Dark Web, 14–15
    DeepSound, 67
    deficiency of, 85
    e-mail, 42
    end-to-end, 41, 42, 106
    hashes, one-way encryption,
        99–100
    keys, 42, 106
    rating, 116
    Steghide, 66
    symmetric, 75, 97–98
    traffic, 41
    Website, 49
    wireless, 100–101
End-to-end encryption, 41, 42, 106
EU biometrics, 39
Evil maid assault, 141
Evil Wiki, 4
EXIF data, 72
EXIF Spider attack, 72
Exploit, 6, 9, 10, 16, 62, 134
    Adobe Flash, 15
    Canvas, 16
    cool, 128

difficult-to-detect exploit software,
17
multiple exploits method, 8
remote, 112
spoofing, 7
vulnerabilities, 12
Eyeball scanners, 38

Facebook, 28
Face scanners, 38
Fancy Bear, cyber espionage group,
84, 93, 94
FinFisher tools, 15
Fingerprint scanners, 38
Forensics, 10, 122
digital, 9
Nmap, 13
Formasaurus, 14
Free Dark Internet search methods,
6
Freenet, 34

Galaxy9
DeadWarrior420, 27–54
GmrB, 64–74
hiring hacker on, 74–75
KelvinSecTeam, 54–64
Galileo tools, 15
GCHQ, 141
GhostNet, 19
The Glass Bead Game, 80
Glorious MrBeast (GmrB)
data encryption, 64–65
DeepSound, 67
digital steganography, 64, 65
LSB process, 65
nMap, data extraction, 72–74
PasteBin, 64
reconnaissance tools, 67–72
Steghide
example, 66
installation, 65–66
stenography, 66–67
WAR file upload, 74
GmrB. See Glorious MrBeast (GmrB)
Google-backed Recorded Future, 5
Grams, 4
Guccifer 2.0, 95

Hacker, 1, 12, 36–37, 88, 91, 92
advertisements, 111
educating and training groups of,
67
GmrB (see Glorious MrBeast
(GmrB))
hiring, 74–75
Internet service provider vendors,
44
non state, 42
Russian, 95
sophisticated hacker classes, 95
targeting DNC, 93
Hacktivist, 1, 104, 111
Hash algorithms, 99
Hashes, 99–100
Hashing, 97, 99, 100
HEX, 75
Hidden Service Prober (HSProbe),
14
Hidden services, 48, 50, 51
Hidden-Web crawler, 108
Hidden Wiki, 2–3, 96
HSProbe. See Hidden Service Prober
(HSProbe)
HTTP/SSL/TLS, 142
"Human hybrid" access, 80

iCloud/Google, 116
Industrial Computer Systems (ICS)
malware
BlackEnergy, 2014, 119
BlackEnergy 2, 2014–2015, 119
facts vs. myth (see Robert M. Lee)
Havex, 2013, 118
Industroyer/Crash Override, 2016,
120
Stuxnet, 2010, 117–118
Triton, 2017, 121–122
Industrial control systems (ICS), 1
Information Security Consortium, 62
Infosec, 122
Internet private investigative
(Internet PI), 56
Interrupted time series (ITS) analysis,
23
Intute, 108
I2P Dark Internet, 7

Jailbreak, 142

Kali Linux OPS, 1, 10–11, 65, 110
Kernel Informed Socket Transport
        (KIST) algorithm, 113
KeyPass backup, 116
Keys, 14, 98, 101
    decryption, 42, 102
    encryption, 42, 106
    long, 105, 106
    registry, 120
    school, 45

LANMAN, 97
Least significant bit (LSB) process,
        65
Lee, Robert M. (ICS)
    accidental attack, 138
    APT, 128
    BTC pipeline, Turkey, 126–127
    circuit breaker system
        vulnerabilities, 135
    Colonel Gardner, 124, 126
    conficker and slammer, 130
    Crash Override, 130, 133, 138
    cyberspace warfare operations
        officer, 122
    DDD ports, 125
    Defence, 136
    defender and intelligence analyst,
        123
    Dragonfly 2.0, 130
    Dragos, Inc., CEO and founder
        of, 122
    education, 122
    e-mail servers and skate
        environments, 129
    HDMI communicates, 135
    ICS network protocols, 134
    Iranian nuclear reactors, 129
    IT security best practices, 137
    Norse cyber attack, 125
    operational risk, 128–129
    Passcode's "Influencers," 122
    physical engineering process, 131
    power grids failure, 123
    ransomware, 128, 131
    Russian cyber attack, 126
    Russian IP address, 124–125
    Sam worm, 130
    skating environment, hijack, 133
    Staples Center, 124
    tradecraft and capabilities, 137
    Ukraine power grid attack, 122,
        132
Linux, 12, 52
    Debian, 77
    Kali, 1, 10, 65, 110
    nMap, 74
    Penetration Testing, 108, 110
Lulz, 143

Maltego, 11
Malware, 6–8, 15, 58, 90
    anti-virus and anti-malware tools, 9
    attacks, 22, 24, 25
    ecosystems, 21, 24
    FinFisher, 15
    detection at NGOs, 21
    families, characterization, 24–25
    ICS (see Industrial Computer
        Systems (ICS) malware)
    sample collection, 59
    Stuxnet, 99
    updates, 9
Man-in-the-middle, 143
MD4, 100
MD5, 100
Memex Project, 13
MetaCarta, 14
Metadata, 95, 108
Metasploit, 11–12
Monas Hieroglyphica, 80
Morphogenetic fields, Sheldrake
        concept of, 81
Mr. Security, 84–96
MVP ends, 37

Network Mapper (Nmap), 12–13
NIST, 97
nMap, data extraction, 72–74
Nonce, 144
Non-Windows hacker tools, 119
Norse cyber attack, 125
Northrop Grumman, 7
NotEvil, 4–5, 108

NSA radar, 35
NSO Pegasus system, 16

Offensive security, 1
Off-The-Record (OTR) plugin, 107
Onion Link, 5
Open-source intelligence (OSINT)
    tools, 1
OpSec, 144

ParrotSec, 110
Passcode's "Influencers," 122
Password cracking, 90
Password managers, 144
Pegasus software, 16–17
Penetration Testing Linux
    distributions, 108, 110
Penetration testing (pentest) software,
    6
PGP. See Pretty Good Privacy (PGP)
PGP encrypted messages, 82
Phishing
    attack, 25, 90, 90, 93
    e-mail, 88, 89, 92, 94, 132
    message, 93
    spear-phishing, 75, 84, 90, 93
PKI. See Public essential infrastructure
    (PKI)
Plaintext, 103
Podesta emails, 84, 85, 96
Pretty Good Privacy (PGP), 9, 82, 84,
    98, 99, 113
Protonmail, 42
Public essential infrastructure (PKI),
    99
Pwned, 145

"Quasi- experimental" design, 23
Qubes, 110

RADIUS. See Remote authentication
    server (RADIUS)
Rail fence cypher, 101
Rainbow table, 146
Ransomware, 22, 128, 131
RAT. See Remote access tool (RAT)
RC4, 98

RCS. See Remote control system
    (RCS)
Reconnaissance tools, 67–72
Red team, 128
Regular phishing, 75
Remote access tool (RAT), 118
Remote authentication server
    (RADIUS), 100
Remote control system (RCS), 15
Rivest, Shamir, and Adleman (RSA),
    98
Robots, 28–30
Root, 29, 82, 127
Rootkit, 15
RSA. See Rivest, Shamir, and
    Adleman (RSA)
Russian cyber attack, 126

Salting, 147
Sam worm, 130
Sandworm, 119, 120
Script kiddies, 138
Search engines, 2–6
SecDev Foundation, 19
SecureWorks, 93
Security budget, 60
Security suites, 6
SHA1, 100
ShadowNet, 19
Shodan, 147–148
Side channel attack, 148
Signature, 99, 104, 111
Slammer, 130
Smoking Gun, 96
Sniffing, 148
Social context, 25
Social engineering, 25
Spear-phishing, 75, 84, 90, 93
Spiders, 28
Spoofing technique, 7, 94
Spyware, 52
SQL injection, 10–11
SQLMap, 10
Startling, 40
Startpage, 112
State actor, 149
Steganography, 64, 65

Steghide
  example, 66
  installation, 65–66
Stenography, 66–67
Straight cable, 74
Substitution-permutation networks,
    103–104
Surface Web, 2
Symmetric cryptography, 97
Symmetric encryption, 75, 97–98

Tails, 50, 52–54
Targeted Threat Index (TTI), 25
TCAP IP protocols, 32, 37
TCP, 75
Technological renaissance, 76, 82–83
Telegram's Super Secret Chats, 116
The Unknowns, 84, 96
Threat Intelligence providers, 58–59
Threat model, 25, 39, 42, 43
3DES, 97
Th Stg. See Cicada 3301, Th Stg
Token, 150
Tor
  anonymity, 33–34
  BitTorrent, 46
  Black Eyed Peas, 44
  browser, 34, 49, 50
  cloud, 34
  CNN dot com, 46–47, 50
  cracking, 38
  darknet, 35–36, 51–52
  definition, 45
  dot onion sites, 48, 50
  geolocation with IP addresses, 46
  hidden services, 48, 50, 51
  hiding location, 46
  multiple proxy servers, 37
  proxy classes, 51
  quicktime flash, 49
  quote-unquote darknet, 51
  relays, 47–49, 51
  routing information, 33
  secret service, 45
  services, 31–33
  Starbucks Wifi VPN, 43
  tails, 50, 52–54

Tor Project dot org, 49
traffic analysis, 46
Trilla, 47
Triola, 47
U.S. Naval Research Laboratory, 45
Tor Browser Bundle, 50
Torch search system, 5, 108
TorSearch, 4
Traffic analysis, 104
TTI. See Targeted Threat Index (TTI)
Two-factor authentication (2FA), 90,
    92
Twofish, 98

UCLA, 108
UDP, 75
Unified Extensible Firmware Interface
    (UEFI), 15
US presidential campaign, 85–96

Verification (ditch), 151
Vigenere, 101
Virtual private networks (VPNs)
  A1d3n, 113
  Black Eyed Peas Tor, 44
  browsing history, 39–40
  Cammi, 43
  confidentiality, 40, 41
  corporate privacy protection, 41
  data encryption, 41
  Eidi, 44
  government's surveillance, 43
  IP address, 39
  ISP advertisers, 42
  jurisdiction, 43
  Kamm's system, 39
  Kubelik origin, 45
  lease lines, 40
  local area networks, 40
  monopolistic Internet service
      provider, 43
  non state hackers, 42
  Privacy Badger cookie, 45
  Protonmail, 42
  sensitive information protection,
      43
  servers, 37

speed data integrity, 40
startling, 40
Virus, 8, 53, 117
VPNs. *See* Virtual private networks
    (VPNs)
Vulnerability (Vuln), 16, 62, 128,
    134, 136, 137
    circuit breaker system, 135
    CyberSAR, 21
    Dark Web site, 11
    Metasploit, 11
    Siemens Patches Vulnerabilities,
    120
    SQL injection, 10
    zero-day, 118
    of Web sites, 57

Walton, Greg
    big data methods, 22–23
    Chinese cyber espionage, 27
    CyberSAR project, 20–21
    data collection, 23
    DNS, 24
    epidemiology, 23–24

malware detection at NGOs, 21
malware families, characterization,
    24–25
Oxford's Cyber Security CDT
    programme, 21
SecDev Foundation, 19–20
third sector *vs.* corporate/
    government sectors, 26
Tibetan NGOs, 19
Warez, 152
WAR files, 74
WEP, 100
Whaling, 90
White hat, 152
Wikileaks, 79, 87, 94, 95
Wireless cryptography, 100–101
WordPress site, 28, 30
Worm, 134
WPA, 100
WPA2-Enterprise, 100
WPA2-PSK, 100

Zero-day, 63, 118
Zeropoint, 21

OTHER TITLES IN OUR BUSINESS LAW AND CORPORATE RISK MANAGEMENT COLLECTION

John Wood, Econautics Sustainability Institute, Editor

- *Preventing Litigation: An Early Warning System to Get Big Value out of Big Data* by Nelson E. Brestoff and William H. Inmon
- *Understanding Consumer Bankruptcy: A Guide for Businesses, Managers, and Creditors* by Scott B. Kuperberg
- *The History of Economic Thought: A Concise Treatise for Business, Law, and Public Policy, Volume I: From the Ancients Through Keynes* by Robert Ashford and Stefan Padfield
- *Buyer Beware: The Hidden Cost of Labor in an International Merger and Acquisition* by Elvira Medici and Linda J. Spievack
- *The History of Economic Thought: A Concise Treatise for Business, Law, and Public Policy, Volume II: After Keynes, Through the Great Recession and Beyond* by Robert Ashford and Stefan Padfield
- *European Employment Law: A Brief Guide to the Essential Elements* by Claire-Michelle Smyth
- *Corporate Maturity and the "Authentic Company"* by David Jackman

Announcing the Business Expert Press Digital Library

Concise e-books business students need for classroom and research

This book can also be purchased in an e-book collection by your library as

- a one-time purchase,
- that is owned forever,
- allows for simultaneous readers,
- has no restrictions on printing, and
- can be downloaded as PDFs from within the library community.

Our digital library collections are a great solution to beat the rising cost of textbooks. E-books can be loaded into their course management systems or onto students' e-book readers.
The **Business Expert Press** digital libraries are very affordable, with no obligation to buy in future years. For more information, please visit **www.businessexpertpress.com/librarians**. To set up a trial in the United States, please email **sales@businessexpertpress.com**.

www.ingramcontent.com/pod-product-compliance
Lightning Source LLC
Chambersburg PA
CBHW061314220326
41599CB00026B/4877

9 781948 976701